Testimonials for Leverage Your Mind

"O.M.G. There are more solid nuggets of self development . . . I mean specific, easy to implement 'how to's' in this book than anything out there. Luc has assembled a uniquely comprehensive treasure trove of wisdom that will help you navigate to a truly evolved life. Could be this generations' Think And Grow Rich!"

David M. Corbin, *Hall of Fame Keynote Speaker—Business Advisor-Award Winning Inventor and Two time bestselling author*

"Luc Goulet and his work are something in and of this world but also reach far beyond what we already know to be true of it. Many leaders promise successful methods to change. But, with ease Luc delivers ways to distinguish yourself from the person you used to know yourself to be with the person and business that you are capable of conceiving, becoming and mastering."

Jo Standing, *Author of* Conquer Trauma Drama, *Speaker and Entertainer on PTSD Resilience*

"In *Leverage Your Mind,* Luc Goulet compassionately delves into the very essence of human suffering and joy, offering his recipe for happiness. It's not the circumstances that we stumble into that transform us. Instead it's our ability to transcend expectations, serve others and choose to fully embrace the whole package of the realities of who we are and what life has to offer with humility and gratitude—the good, the bad and the ugly, that creates the change we seek."

Dr. Theresa Nicassio, *Registered Psychologist & Integrative Wellness Educator, Award-Winning Author of* YUM: Plant-Based Recipes for a Gluten-Free Diet *& Founder of TheresaNicassio.com*

"Leverage your mind" is a game changer! Word for word, this book is filled with empowering messages to inspire us to live life to the fullest. I was inspired by Luc's first book "The Big Bang Project", however in this book, Luc takes it to the next level and shows us step by step, how to open our hearts, believe with 100% conviction that whatever we want to achieve is waiting for us.

If you need to be inspired, or need an injection of confidence and belief in your next project, this book shines! Luc has an honourable gift with his writing, reaching out via his heart. His words literally lifted from the pages and found their way to me on a soul level. "Leverage your mind" is a book everyone must read! Read this book today, and see the results of your new life unfold right before your very eyes."

Jason Stephenson, *You Tube meditation superstar with over 60 million views and 500,000 followers. CEO, Relax Me Online Australia Pty Ltd*

When Luc Goulet says "Happiness is choice and success is a mindset" he masterfully captures the essence of how to live a more joyful, wholehearted life. His book *Leverage Your Mind* is all about how to "reset" not only the old, self-defeating patterns of thinking, perceiving and being but also those beliefs and cognitions that do not serve to move us into joyful and abundant living. Here is a jewel of a book, concise, accessible, easy to read and yet profound in terms of powerful insights and tools to create the life we truly wish to lead. I highly recommend this book as it seems to me to be a guiding light in the current darkness of confusion, fear and uncertainty around us.

> **Robert (Dusty) Staub**, *author of 4 books including the best selling* The 7 Acts of Courage *and more than 300 articles on human systems excellence, is President of Staub Leadership International a consulting firm dedicated to creating abundance in organizations and life by liberating the Purpose, Passion and Power of individuals, teams and organizations.*

"Luc Goulet has not only given the right tools needed to achieve the desired life worth living in success, happiness and inner core fulfillment, he has also touched upon the relevance of human emotions and the importance of cultivating and reprograming your thinking for your true purpose in your life journey. I can't emphasize enough how valuable this book can be for one's purpose towards self-empowerment and reaching their desired goals with life transformation and peace. This is an absolute must read."

> **Dr. Bindu Babu**, *I-MD, PHD*

"As a professional tennis coach, I highly recommend Leverage Your Mind to all coaches, teachers, mentors, athletes and students. The peak performance mindset techniques put forth will help you reach your personal level of excellence. This is priceless information for anyone who wants to perform at their best, always!"

> **François Lefebvre**, *Top level professional tennis coach*

Praise for The Big Bang Project:

"The Big Bang Project is about global transformation with Success, with a capital "S", underscored in gold with lots of bright lights! Here's an opportunity to take part and participate in creating a world that does work. Read this book, get involved!"

Jack Canfield, *Author of "Chicken Soup For The Soul"*
and world renowned speaker and mentor

"What an amazing book! What incredible insight from Luc Goulet. If you've ever hoped for change for the positive in our hectic world, then look no further than this book. I read this book over 2 nights. It has inspired me so much. It's a true 'wake up!' for us all. If you would like to purchase yourself only ONE BOOK this year, please do yourself a favour and grab this book by Luc. It is LIFE CHANGING!"

"This is a Powerful, Powerful book! It summed-up what I always longed for in this world"

Jason Stephenson, *You Tube meditation superstar with over 60 million views and 500,000 followers. CEO, Relax Me Online Australia Pty Ltd*

"*The Big Bang Project*, by Entrepreneur, Coach, and Author, **Luc Goulet**, is a totally inspirational and logical approach to "Creating Humanity's Best-Case Scenario. Listen, as Nick, and author Goulet discuss the need for new thinking in the areas of Capitalism, Democracy and Religion. Goulet believes in the power of "me to we and from we to me". In other words, instead of fighting and division, in religion and politics, we need to establish harmony, cooperation and respect for each other's differences, so that we all grow and prosper. This book and interview are truly a "keeper", that you'll want to enjoy over-and-over again!"

Andrew Flores, *This week's Straight Talk with Nick Lawrence*

★★★★★ Amazon reviews:

"If your vision doesn't scare you it's not big enough.", February 7, 2017

This is a big picture perspective book. The quote "If your vision doesn't scare you it's not big enough," (Angus Buchan), applies to this book. The author stirs the mind and the soul and asks questions of what each of us corporately and individually can contribute in our own way to improve the lot of all humanity. The book provides plenty of suggestions.

It doesn't pretend to have answers but does ask us to take responsibility to work towards solutions. With just over 100 pages it is a relatively easy read. The book is well-written, well structured and well laid out.

A recommended read to all that would want the best for our planet and its inhabitants.

By Gazman
Format: Kindle Edition
5.0 out of 5 stars **A fantastic beginning of a transformational movement!**

This is not only a visionary's treatise on how we can, finally, create a world that works for all, but it is a blueprint of living a life that is big, beautiful and of service to others. What more could we want? Mr. Goulet has the courage to embrace the totality of what this world has and proposes a way to harness it all, come together as community and create something that is bigger and better than what we have had and than what we could have imagined as single individuals.

The Big Bang Project has the potential to be a movement of power and grace in our world. If we each throw in our hat, we can make it happen!

By LCS on December 20, 2016
5.0 out of 5 stars **Thanks Luc. It's about time someone wrote a book like yours with hope for all!**

"An inspiring and instructional book that gives hope and can help us be the best humans we can be to achieve the best possible outcomes in our crazy world we live in. We need to learn to share better, so we can all enjoy the fruits and benefits of our Mother Earth equally. His down to earth look into what is wrong with our world and how to fix it are right on. The book is well written, easy to understand and bipartisan. Let's hope that with Luc's help, we can create humanity's Best-Case Scenario. Otherwise we will all suffer for it. Thanks for the great book and insights. I hope to use quotes from you in my book on why we need a green revolution and put our money where our hearts are. Wishing you the best success for your book, endeavors and life for the holidays and New Year!"

By Allan on November 25, 2015
5.0 out of 5 stars **A Life changing book. THANK YOU!!!**

"This book reassures you that there is a hint of good in everybody you meet. When you live life from a perspective of service, you will be guided to succeed in extraordinary feats, and I am grateful I have read this book to remind me of that!"

By Jo Standing on March 9, 2017
5.0 out of 5 stars **Embrace, Explore, Evolve!**

"Finally—a book that helps people to imagine possibilities so we can raise our personal standards, ask the right questions and strategically take the right actions to be part in the evolution of humanity's best-case scenario. In a world of confusion where most people feel powerless, here comes a book that not only motivates and inspires us to believe that change is good and that we can change! As we reset our standards, to no longer accept mediocrity and our inability to express our views on very critical issues, we are now able to participate in conversations on how we can all reinvent ourselves to become the truly evolved species we aspire to be! Embrace potential, explore possibilities, so we can all evolve to our highest and best! Luc's background and life's experiences are simply remarkable. This book is not theory, this is analysis, facts and inspiration in action. A highly compelling book which I am definitely gifting to my family and friends!"

By Emma Tiebenson November 16, 2015

Leverage Your Mind

THE NEXT PHASE IN SELF-EMPOWERMENT: A BETTER ME FOR A BETTER WE

By Luc Goulet

Published by
Union Square Publishing

Union Square Publishing
301 E. 57th Street, 4th floor
New York, NY 10022
www.unionsquarepublishing.com

Copyright © 2017 by Luc Goulet

All rights reserved. No part of this book may be reproduced or transmitted in any form or by in any means, electronic or mechanical, including photocopying, recording, or by any information storage and retrieval system, without the written permission of the Publisher, except where permitted by law.

Manufactured in the United States of America, or in the United Kingdom when distributed elsewhere.

Library of Congress Control Number: 2017951917

Goulet, Luc
Leverage Your Mind
ISBN:
Paperback: 978-1-946928-06-1
eBook: 978-1-946928-07-8

Cover design by: Joe Potter
Interior design: Scribe, Inc
Photo credits: ThinkStock / www.thinkstockphoto.com, Luc Goulet

www.leverageyourmind.com

ACKNOWLEDGMENTS

Thank you so much to the extraordinary team of Union Square Publishing for making it real: Rick Frishman, Scott Frishman, Adam Giandomenico, and Karen Strauss. I'm eternally grateful. Many thanks to Justin Spizman, my book architect.

I'm very privileged to have had incredible mentors who helped me pave the path to my vision and mission. Thank you so much to the team of Algorithms for Success, which has supported my efforts from day one: Adam Giandomenico, Starley Murray, Keoki Williams, and Perry Yeldham. The team at Quantum Leap got me started on the right foot, thank you so much: Steve Harrison, Geoffrey Berwind, and all the great coaches. Emma Tiebens, you are awesome! To all my amazing colleagues and friends: Judith Trustone, Jason Stephenson, Jos Madelaine Standing, Dr. Bhoja Katipally, Dr. Bindu Babu, Gary Stone, Leeza Steindorf, Richard Crawford, Atta Arghandiwal, Bill Hargenrader, Jennifer Hammond, Dusty Staub, Peter Hobler, Dr. Theresa Nicassio, and so many more.

My journey allowed me to meet incredibly successful people. They all made a huge impact in my mission. I'm privileged to have encountered such amazing human beings whose greatness and generosity surpass even their financial success or fame: Jack Canfield, Kevin Harrington, George Flinn, Patty Auberry, Greg Jacobson, David Corbin, Alex Carroll, and again, Rick Frishman, and Steve Harrison.

To my friend and great tennis coach, François Lefebvre, thank you for letting me work with your son, Vincent, an incredible young elite tennis player.

Of course, my beautiful family is largely responsible for executing my dream. Nancy, Vincent, and Philippe, I love you profoundly. Thanks to my brother, Claude, and his beautiful wife, Sylvie. Linda, my sister, and her husband, Claude Lorange. My amazing nieces Joanie, Marie Pier, and Jacinthe, I love you all.

Thank you to the CQCD (Conseil Québécois du Commerce de Détail), "The Retail Council of Quebec", for giving our family business, Panda Shoes, a Lifetime Achievement Award for our contribution to the retail scene in Quebec. It was an extraordinary honor that represents the value of teamwork and perseverance. Thank you to every franchisee, manager, and employee who has been part of Panda Shoes throughout the years. This prize belongs to you too.

Thank you to the media: Maggie Linton, Kimberly Crawford, Nick Lawrence, Melodee Meyer. My first interviews happened because of you trusting me. Thank you in advance to all media spreading the word.

Last but not least, thank YOU for wanting to continually better yourself as a human being. I wrote this book for you. You are in my tribe. May the journey I propose in this work help you achieve your dream life.

TABLE OF CONTENTS

Introduction	vii
Chapter 1: Leverage Your Mind: *The Evolution That Leads to a Revolution*	1
The Paradigm Shift: Happiness Is Your Choice, Success Is Your Mindset	1
Era of Rapid Evolution: The Next Phase in Self-Empowerment	6
The Great Influence of Suggestion	11
My Four Hidden Aces	15
No More Excuses! The 3R Approach for Success	22
Chapter 2: Recognize: *Expand Your Mind— Debunk Your Limiting Beliefs*	25
Our Minds Have Been Hacked	25
The Massive Devastation of Negativity	28
Maximize Your Potential, Reach Beyond "Set Limits"	31
Recognizing the Key Factors of Success	33
Chapter 3: Reset Your Mindset: *Where Do We Begin?*	35
Turning Negative into Positive: A Conscious Effort	35
Premises for Success	36
Getting the Negative Out for Good: Five Easy Visualization Tricks	38
Chapter 4: Digging Deeper to Reset: *How to Speak and Influence the Subconscious*	47
Power Programming by Self-Hypnosis	48
Meditation: Connecting with Your Inner Peace	56
Magnetize to Receive Positive Energy	58
Wild Cards for a Perfect Hand	60

Chapter 5: Recognize and Reset for Complete
    Success in All Aspects of Life 67
The Humble Human Perspective:
    Recognize Your Greatness 67
Reset Your Invincible Self-Esteem:
    Bring on the Bullies 69
Reset Your Relationships 71
Success and Wealth; Recognize and
    Own the Key Factors of Success 73
Reset Your Mindset and Lifestyle 78
Reset Your Inner Peace and Fulfillment 81
Confront Your Demons 83

Chapter 6: Reinvent: *Concrete Actions*
    for Concrete Results 85
What Now? 85
Key Factors of Success 87
Reinventing Your Mind: New
    Actions Create New Habits 88
Peak Performance Secrets to Be Your Best 92
Peak Performance: From Mind to Action 94

Chapter 7: The Next Level of Self-Empowerment:
    A Better ME for a Better WE 99
Leveraging OUR Possibilities: *The 3R*
    for Social Repair 99
Magnetizing the Energy of Kindness
    to Reset Globally 101
What You Can Do for Your Country
    Will Also Benefit You 103
Individual Responsibilities 103
When Positive Forces Unite: A Grand Explosion
    of Good in Your Neighborhood 109

Conclusion: *Be the Change You Want to See* 115

INTRODUCTION

Your life is the result of the reality you have created in your mind, heart, and soul. It is in part based on how you perceive yourself, what you know and decide to learn, what you believe, what you feel, what you want, what you fear, and what you do with all this information and insight. Your reality is a creation of your mind. Actions start with a thought, an idea, and a feeling, combined with intention. These are all the product of a complicated mental process involving your brain, heart, and soul.

The brain alone is the path to align the conscious mind to the subconscious mind.

Happiness is a choice, and success is a mindset. The secret is knowing how to **leverage your mind**. You can train your brain to get what you want, then learn to align it with your subconscious, and use your heart and soul to **recognize your greatness**, your unlimited potential, and your unique skills and experiences. Then you **reset within** by reprogramming with only the positive perspective, always disregarding negative thoughts and feelings. Last, you **reinvent yourself** through your actions. That is the path of pursuit to recognize a remarkable life.

They say that if you repeat the same actions, you will have the same results. So how can you reprogram your mind to make those changes that you want and create your desired reality?

Here's the good news: You can reprogram yourself, your thoughts, your beliefs, your emotions, your behavior, even your actions at will. It might seem difficult, but the tools in this book will help make it easy. Your subconscious will believe what you want it to believe. You just need to know how to "speak" directly to it. I will show you how to do that.

The ultimate **self-empowerment** approach is to become the **master** of your mind and the **mastermind** of your life. That's what *Leveraging Your Mind* is all about.

What does "leverage" mean? To leverage something is simply to take everything you have at your disposal and create maximum growth by utilizing their combined forces and capabilities. That is the goal of this book: To offer you the self-empowerment techniques to mold your reality as you wish and ultimately take full control and responsibility for your success.

Two important reasons are behind why this work represents *the next phase in Self-Empowerment.*

The first reason: These important self-programming tools and techniques are presented in one book. This singular resource guide will help you literally put it all together. From concepts to easy-to-use applications, enabling you to tap on your own into your full potential. This book will help you achieve perfect alignment: You will learn how to suggest what you want at every level of your being—from your conscious, to subconscious, to feelings, and emotions. You will learn how to connect with your inner soul too. You will own and always carry with you the ultimate winning hand, **four aces,** and many **wild cards** from which you can choose. The four aces—**visualization, self-hypnosis, meditation,** and **magnetism**—and their supporting resources are proven methods that work. Individually, these mind-controlling techniques are very powerful. Their combined power is limitless. You will learn to use them to discard negativity, conquer challenges, and achieve many of your goals and dreams. You will find your inner peace by tapping into the far depth of your mind and soul. You can then possess the tools to forge your reality as you want it to be.

The second benefit of this book: It will help you reach the next level of self-empowerment, which comes in the form of the great personal rewards of connecting positively with people and the universe. Once you do that, you will be more in tune with the energy surrounding you and eventually become a better human being. You can then emit, receive, and harness only positive energy. By contributing to a better WE, you also empower yourself, therefore becoming a better ME.

You will also learn the **3R action plan**, which consists of **recognizing** what you really want and the **key factors of success** to get there. You can then **reset your mindset** and **reprogram** all levels of your mind, using the right method(s). Finally, you'll **reinvent through action** and secure a clear action plan to take concrete steps forward and create your new routine in less than thirty days.

The results can be tremendous, and you will begin a cycle of continual improvement and progress. The long-lasting benefits will always follow you and increase with time.

In the past few years, science has evolved in regard to understanding the mind. Our true reality is very far from three dimensional and it far exceeds our five senses. Our universe is full of energy fields, magnetic frequencies, and many dimensions.

I will offer you a unique perspective that connects all the dots, where science, spirituality, psychology, and even religion meet. I have simplified the concepts and applications so that anybody can benefit from the methods proposed. These steps will help you improve many spheres of your life, including wealth, success, health, and your overall well-being.

Open your mind, your heart, and your soul to this extraordinary journey. I offer you nothing less than a life-transformative experience. Become the best possible you. Find out your best-case scenario and enjoy!

CHAPTER 1

Leverage Your Mind
The Evolution That Leads to a Revolution

The Paradigm Shift: Happiness Is Your Choice, Success Is Your Mindset

We are all on a constant quest for happiness and success. Who doesn't want to be happy? But only a few of us will put in the hard work to achieve that lofty goal. So many things can get in the way . . . like life!

While you may think success is an initial requirement to reach some semblance of happiness, that isn't always the case. Most people will change their definition of success by always seeking new goals and then postponing their true goal of simply being happy. Along the way, some people celebrate great success but even then are not fully happy.

When we see happy people living in very poor conditions, some of us become more confused. How can these people be content with so little? Then comparatively speaking, some people's success might be the definition of failure for others. It all just seems so relative, with no rhyme, reason, or explanation.

Of course, life circumstances will have an important impact on your happiness. What you do about those specifics and how you evolve from challenges and hardships remains your choice. It all rests on your mindset. Our reaction to different stimuli, positive or negative, is often manifested by instinct, which is a preset mental programming. This is a result of how your whole being has registered cumulative information you've received since birth. Your brain interacts with your conscious, subconscious, and unconscious. Feelings and emotions are added to the equation, and your genes certainly play an important role. The mind then tries to interpret different information from many sources, creating many conflicting responses.

Our environment is another important player in our success and happiness. What happens to us, how it happens, with whom it happens, and even where it happens all impact our ability to find true and lasting happiness. We still have our personal part to play in many of the what, how, when, and where things happen to us. Does this mean that happiness is a choice? There certainly is an argument for that notion.

Dictionaries say happiness is "an emotional state of well-being defined by a positive emotion ranging from contentment to intense joy." Think about that for a second. Emotions are subjective and can therefore vary according to your interpretation as well as how you express them. So if we program, or reprogram, our mindset, we could have an intentional influence on the amount and intensity of our emotions in a good or bad way. We can then deduce that this state of well-being can be experienced for a very short moment to a prolonged period or even become a constant within our lives. It is like hearing a song you like, and depending on your mood or desire to hear it, turning the volume up or down. A mental setting can help you prolong the moments of happiness and reduce the duration of the negative thoughts and the effects on your state of mind.

But the key to all of this is to understand exactly how emotions are created and managed. That's the choice you need to make. After we learn the best methods to create a positive mindset, we can then live in a constant state of joy, fulfillment, gratitude, and appreciation of every moment. That is the goal of this book.

Success is really the result of the actions you take to reach your goals. All actions start with thoughts manifested within our minds, which are then guided by very specific knowledge and emotions. Planning our actions ahead with method and clear purpose can make all the difference. But in the end, *your mindset determines your actions.* You must change your mindset if you want to recognize better actions in order to reach desired goals and dreams. You choose what you decide to learn and what you decide to do about it.

Making a conscious choice to change is the starting point. That is why you purchased this book. But there's more to it than that. You can't just pick up a book, put it under your pillow, and expect immediate and substantial change. You need to communicate your intentions of change to other layers of your mind. Your subconscious might disagree. Your feelings and emotions could even play tricks on you. This explains why most attempts to change take far too long or end up failing in the long run.

Consider the following statistics:

- 98 percent of people can't lose weight.
- 85 percent of relationships fail.
- 18 percent of people suffer from anxiety and/or depression.
- 20 percent of people suffering from anxiety or depression are addicted to something they wish they were not.
- 67 percent of people feel they're not making the money they deserve.
- 9 out of 10 business start-ups fail.[1]

While these numbers might vary from one study to another, they reveal a rather sad picture of our general sense of well-being, success, and overall state of happiness.

---
[1] https://www.nimh.nih.gov/index.shtml

Could this be an indicator that most proposed "cures" don't really work? The magic pill for solving all your problems and giving you the perfect life doesn't yet exist. Don't hold your breath—unlike a computer, we are not equipped with a simple reset button that may purge our internal system of all that ails us. We just don't have an option for a "hard reset." Psychologists are doing their best to help, but the results are somewhat limited simply because their approach is somewhat limited. So as not to diminish their abilities, the fact remains that they offer strong arguments and advice to convince only one part of your mind—your conscious. They will most likely find the right diagnosis, but the solution they propose with prescription pills and continued conversation can only reduce the symptoms while resulting in side effects that could make the initial problem worse. It is like a band-aid that will always need to be replaced. I propose something to make their suggestions much more powerful, lasting, and meaningful—a process of positive life change consisting of five steps that I call the **Perfect Five Alignment**. The steps are:

1. **Know it.** Learn the key factors of success for any challenge from the best possible mentors. Know how, and know you can.
2. **Believe it.** Communicate the most powerful positive messages to your subconscious so you believe you can, to the core of your mind.
3. **Do it.** Be the victor through actions, stumble forward, improve each time. You now have proof that you can do it.
4. **Feel it.** Feel the moment and the positive emotions, and with every success feel the new you.
5. **Be it.** It now becomes second nature. Be all you want to be by repeating the process for any goal or challenge.

This book focuses on the journey toward achieving real happiness and true success. That is my promise to you. Together we can shift the paradigm by helping you better understand how your mind works to create your ideal reality. Your mind is responsible for your successes, failures, emotions, actions, and even your life.

The goal is to *make your life your success*, while enjoying happiness as an automatic outcome. Success is not a measurement of happiness. Some people would tell you they don't correlate at all. Think about all the people who have a great job with plenty of money but remain miserable on the inside and the outside. This paradigm shift changes how you will get there. The strategy is different because we consider all the aspects for a complete mindset evolution. These are done in perfect sequence, instead of being measured only by one or a few elements. Motivators might successfully pump you up through offering their best tricks at getting rich, but this energy often fizzles once they leave the stage. It just doesn't reach deep enough to register in your subconscious and spiritual levels. It is like eating sugar—a quick high followed by a momentous crash. But if you program your core to have a great life, you will begin to understand a global perspective rather than a narrow set of reasons to be happy or not. By mobilizing yourself for greatness, you can reprogram your whole being to be constantly motivated by your life. This goes deep to your core, into your roots, and your DNA.

I do not offer you any promise, simply because the ultimate results depend on your choice to apply the knowledge put forth in this work. Your hard work will create your happiness. But the ideas and proposed solutions work. If we reunite the different expertise and organize them in a step-by-step plan, we can achieve just about anything. The choice to reach the mindset for happiness and success is yours, so long as you are ready to do the work to reshape your own view of life.

Era of Rapid Evolution: The next phase in Self-Empowerment

Social revolutions start with individual evolution. The equation is quite simple: I call it a better ME for a better WE, and a Better WE for a better ME. The more successful you are, the better you are equipped to help others. By the same token, the happier and better off your family, friends, and community are, the greater likelihood of your own success and happiness. Let's unpack this concept of how our happiness impacts the overall happiness of our world.

Connecting with one another is crucial for our well-being. The greatest torture we can imagine is being left in "the hole" with no contact with anyone for a long period. In contrast, *the best feel good of all* is the emotion offered by kindness. Knowing the importance of your part in the social transformation is also understanding how the rewards come back to you. With the technologies of communication today, we are closer than ever before to considering the following: "Ask yourself not what your country can do for you, but ask what you can do for your country." To do so, first determine what you can do to better yourself, from personal empowerment, to getting to the next level, to local commitment, and then from local commitment to global impact. This is a great opportunity for all of us to take advantage of this possibility of being our own hero. Being part of the solution and having a sense of meaning and fulfillment is part of being the best you can be. Our joined positive energies and actions can turn the worldwide tide of negativity around so that we can produce a better world.

Our world is extremely different today than it was just a few decades ago. We have enjoyed major advancements in the fields of science and technology, which continue to change right before our very eyes. We should consider ourselves fortunate to witness this incredible time of rapid evolution. It offers possibilities like never before. The capacity to instantly communicate on a global scale is quickly bringing the world much closer together. We all now have access to extreme amounts of information with just the click of a button.

This new reality offers us the opportunity to know more and learn more than ever before. These technological advancements and our ability to share them with the world triggers a social and individual revolution. We are at a historical stage, and there is a worldwide consensus that we can use these resources for great change. This is a critical phase of evolution. We have the power to influence our lives, our community, and even have a global impact through using the resources available to each of us.

The younger generations are already much more open to different cultures and much more aware of the world around them. They instantly search and find information and can then use that acquired knowledge to leave imprints in their pathway and along their journeys.

Science has taken giant leaps in the study and understanding of the brain and mind in the past few years. More than ever, we can now observe and study our mind and its capacity. The incredible precision and accuracy of modern instruments, not available only a few decades ago, have confirmed theories about our energy and its link to our well-being. For example, we can monitor, visualize, and measure our brain activity with methods such as "functional magnetic resonance imaging" (fMRI), "magnetoencephalography" (MEG), and "electroencephalography" (EEG). Each of these tools measures and visualizes brain activity by monitoring magnetic frequencies in different forms. Today, we can see the electromagnetic fields we emit, how they fluctuate with our mood, and how they alter the surrounding electromagnetic frequencies.

It is completely fascinating to explore our brain with today's advanced equipment. Just a few years ago, the brain could only be studied post-mortem, with no present activity. Now we can analyze a living brain and use imagery to understand its real-time reaction to various situations and stimuli. We can identify and scale frequencies emitted by our brain as well as their connection to our overall state of mind.

This capacity to explore the mind leads us to unexpected discoveries that prove we have the inner power to reprogram ourselves and achieve what seemed impossible before. Studying our brain allows us to further understand how it impacts our happiness and overall success. By tapping into all layers of the mind, we can control our memory, our focus, our mood, and our mental and physical performances. We can turn our worst fears and phobias into our biggest strengths. By simply changing our perception of reality on a deeper level, we now can confirm that you change your reality.

We are starting to challenge traditional medicine with concepts it always refuted, like energy healing, acupuncture, brain wave emitters, and the power of positive programming. The field of quantum physics has made giant leaps in the study of magnetic frequencies. Our comprehension of the energy our body radiates and how it can be influenced by our state of mind is greater than ever before. People like monks, yogis, healers, and martial arts experts have maintained a constant awareness and have used this energetic power within. It was only in the 1980s that Dr. John Zimmerman, at the University of Colorado, used a superconducting quantum interface device (SQUID), to discover that our bodies produce a bio-magnetic field. This extremely precise instrument measures the frequencies we emit. The frequencies have the same range as our own brain waves, from 0.3 HZ to 30 HZ (cycles per second). What seemed impossible now has the scientific community re-evaluating its approach to health and well-being.

The many links between our conscious, subconscious, body, heart, and soul are now evident. They all impact the journey through success and our arrival at happiness. The methods to find your inner strengths are now proven facts. The link between science, psychology, theory, philosophy, religions, and spirituality is clearer than ever before. Our comprehension of our world impacts our understanding of the possibilities available to us. From the smallest atoms, our genome, to our better knowledge about our universe, recent discoveries reveal a new reality in many dimensions.

We have discovered that energy fields are present between every atom. Our neurons communicate in energy pulses and frequencies. The Air Force concluded an experiment held in the 1980s and reported its findings to *Nature* magazine in May 1986. They concluded that empty space is far from empty. There are many levels and dimensions of magnetic frequencies and more. Everything is linked by energetic frequencies. The scientific community has come to consensus about this energy between all matter. The most common names that describe this observation are "the field" and the "matrix." While all religions believe in a god, science now believes in the field. I like to call it the "Grid of Dimensions," where all nonphysical and physical dimensions co-exist and are linked by this endless energy grid. I also like the "coincidence" that the acronym for my definition is "GOD."

Very few people are aware of these incredible findings simply because many industries rely on you not knowing. Of course, they represent many billions of dollars in potential loss of profit for many large corporations that sell cures you might not need. This offers us the opportunity to evolve like never before.

Leveraging your mind simply means maximizing your capabilities to your fullest potential by using every resource at your disposal. I aim to demystify, simplify, and connect all the dots about how normal people like you and me can use these discoveries to be happy. I devoted my research to use these findings for self-empowerment and to show you how to make them part of your normal routine. You will learn easy methods to immediately shift your perspective from negative to positive and confront your fears and challenges with your head up, knowing that you are capable and will grow by confronting them.

Imagine knowing all the important "secrets" of experts in different areas, which are then presented in a way you could use for any purpose and at anytime. You could use a combination of skills to achieve results you never dreamed of before. A level of flexibility and adaptability like never before would ensue.

In this book, I will also show the benefits of peak-performance mental techniques and exercises used by elite athletes, which enable them to reach new limits. In sports, all the top players maintain a certain level of mental toughness. While most will master the physical or the technical and tactical facets of the game, the greatest athletes have learned that mindset control makes all the difference. The advanced scientific research proves that the mindset skills taught by peak-performance coaches have a great impact on performance. These coaches are part of Olympic training teams for the best professional athletes in the world. That's because the stakes are huge: There are many contenders, so they need to achieve their best results at the perfect moment.

Our journey together is also based on maximizing your performance in all you do. Learning to apply peak-performance mental techniques can serve you in many aspects of life. How you mentally prepare to better perform in all circumstances will greatly increase your chances of success in your career, your relationships, and in dealing with adversity.

Thanks to studies conducted by experts like Dr. David Williams, professor of African and African American Studies and Sociology at Harvard University, we now understand that we have a predisposed bias about ethnicities and races. He revealed his findings at the 2012 Kellogg Conference, ten years after the subject was first put forth at the same conference. The damaging effect of negative messages repeated over generations has influenced our perception of other races, cultures, and backgrounds. This is called unconscious bias, and it means we have incorrectly bought into limiting beliefs and messages. We judge without really knowing. It is instinctual. Our perception of others and ourselves is altered at a deep level, and this explains how deep we must go into our conscious and subconscious to undo the negative programming we are all "victims" of.

This is just one example of how people start to believe false and damaging information and then spread it to others. It should be our mission to turn this tide of negativity into positive and peaceful solutions. The great news is that it is easier than you think. You just need to know how a few changes in behavior can make a huge impact on your life.

We also know how to change negative thoughts into positive ones. Debunking the myths about your limits changes your outlook on your possibilities. It arms you with an invincible self-esteem, humility, courage, and understanding to allow you to mentally deal with any challenge.

Fast-pace evolution is the best trigger for a rapid revolution. Sharing evolutionary ideas on a large scale can create global revolutions. Everything is being requestioned and reevaluated, socially, politically, environmentally—even the ethical questions about our scientific discoveries.

Science is not the focus of this book, but it does serve to support the methods proposed to reprogram yourself spiritually, physically, mentally, and emotionally. There's nothing new about these techniques, but what is new is our ability to verify the knowledge we have obtained through many sources. Now we know for sure what works and what doesn't. This book scours and then presents some of the easiest techniques for self-reprogramming in a way that complements their true value and purpose. Separately the four mindset methods (the "Four Aces") outlined in the upcoming chapters, have proven wonders, but when combined the possibilities are practically limitless.

The Great Influence of Suggestion

The message in the forthcoming chapters is far from rocket science. This book presents simple—even ancient—methods used by people across the world. I will facilitate their applications in an easy-to-learn and use format. You will learn to use them in a step-by-step progression for lasting results.

It all begins with a very simple and powerful concept: **the great influence of suggestion.** When you grasp the profound meaning of this idea, you can then suggest whatever you want to your mind. Let's explain this concept in greater detail. We are molded by endless suggestions from our parents, friends, society, advertising, and more. These suggestions enter our minds at different levels of consciousness. They are reinforced by repetition, enabling them to have an even deeper effect on our psyche. It becomes the nature versus nurture conversation. But what's beautiful is that they can be replaced by positive custom-made new suggestions, and you can manage your reprogramming in the process. Forget the Freudian approach to dig into your past to find the source of your problem or trauma. You don't need to undo the past. The past is part of the journey. Rather, you must instead substitute your programming with new messages that focus on your positive future. This is much easier and takes far less time.

Our brain is absolutely fascinating. Thanks to the accuracy of the equipment used ("EEG" electroencephalogram), as seen in the graphic below, we can clearly identify and measure the frequencies of electrical currents our minds use to communicate information between our neurons. These brain waves represent the different state of consciousness that operate in symbiosis. Through imagery, we can see how our brains react to different stimuli in all areas of our mind.

You will learn how to reach your conscious, subconscious, unconscious, and even your spiritual awareness. The five major categories of range of frequencies, from the very deep sleep to a super state of consciousness, include:

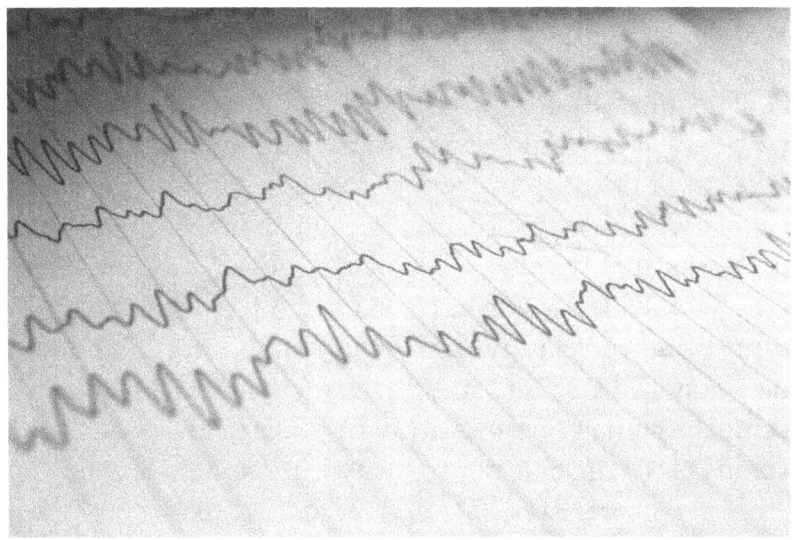

1. Delta (0.5–3.9 Hz): associated with very deep dreamless sleep, deep into the unconscious mind or "supra-consciousness."
2. Theta (4–7.9 Hz): associated with light sleep (REM dream state), deep meditation, intuition, and subconscious mind.
3. Alpha (8–13.9 Hz): known as "gateway" to the subconscious, associated with deep relaxation, and light meditation, where creativity and "super learning" is at its maximum.
4. Beta (14–30 Hz): associated with the normal waking state of consciousness, alertness, concentration, focus, and our five physical senses.
5. Gamma (30–100 Hz): associated with a higher state of consciousness.

These are measured in hertz (in cycles per second), like electric currents. Every mindset-control method involves reaching the deeper layers of consciousness. It's easy to get there thanks to simple suggestions and visualization techniques presented in this book. Most of the techniques used for resetting your mindset are most effective in an easy to reach state of relaxation. The gateway to our receptive subconscious brain waves is just below a normal relaxed state. The magic of reprogramming occurs in the alpha (very accessible), and theta, the range you can get with a bit of practice with the right techniques. Many tricks involve the conscious mind as a key player, still "awake" while being also very relaxed. The idea is to gradually get your mind to relax with the right suggestions. The process is quite easy to learn and master. Your mind can still be aware consciously while communicating to deeper levels of your subconscious. So you can consciously choose what your deeper layers hear and register.

Next, we need to find the perfect suggestions for our specific goal and the most efficient ways to communicate them to all levels of our mind, spirit, and body so that you can speak more directly to your subconscious. For best results, you will know how to create the best conditions for your subconscious to be receptive to your suggestions. This allows you to connect on a spiritual level with ease, tapping only into the positive energy within you and surrounding you.

Finally, we can implement an easy-to-follow plan that produces results without compromising our daily routine. This process culminates in inviting self-serving suggestions that can move you in the direction of your true success and inevitable happiness.

Maintaining a desire to become rich and famous may not be the right tactic to achieve that desire. For example, if you're a singer or actor, aiming to be the best you can be at your art form will likely serve you better than merely a hope and a dream. *Asking the right question is far better than getting a good answer to a bad question.* So determining what you truly want requires some profound introspection. Searching for the cause of your bad emotions is one thing, but more importantly, you must search for ways to transform this energy into positive thinking. You really need to focus on your true passions, skills, goals, and motivators.

My Four Hidden Aces

Now, you must learn a few basic skills that will help you reset your mindset. I call them the **four hidden aces**. Each of these can help influence you in many ways. But when combined, their impact is even greater. Let's unpack the most powerful ways to take full control of your life. The four hidden aces allow me to make my positive suggestions really sink in from a conscious, to subconscious, to an emotional, and at a spiritual level.

Ace #1) Visualization: We begin by recognizing and visualizing the best suggestions for you. This is a conscious exercise that becomes the starting point of mind transformation. You will learn how to use visualization tricks and other ways to reinforce positive messages. Our brain remembers images much more than words or even numbers. When your mind associates something with an image, it will remember it much more easily and for a longer time. It is fascinating to see how a trained mind can remember almost anything using this technique. In America, there's a growing discipline that has been popular in Asia for a long time. It consists of memorizing a shuffled full deck of cards from the first card to the last in just a few minutes. Asians have mastered this discipline and are the best in the world at it. They invent and visualize a story where each card is associated with an image that fits in their story. In their minds, they create ultra-unique images that become easy to remember.

Throughout this book, we will use visualization to reinforce positive thoughts. The first part consists of easy tricks to reprogram all negative thoughts and emotions into a positive reality. We will then see how these techniques can greatly improve your focus, memory, self-esteem, and so much more. If you fear missing something, you send a negative suggestion focused on the word "missing." If you visualize yourself perfectly exercising a task or decision, the positive visualization will significantly improve your chances of success.

Again, a small twist can make all the difference. For example, let's say you want to purchase a dream car. Some would suggest visualizing that car in your garage, or even putting posters of the car in your office and bedroom. But I would submit to you it is stronger to visualize the image of seeing yourself as the person who can own any car he wants. Self-esteem and our perception of our capabilities is largely the result of the image we create of ourselves.

Ace #2) Self-Hypnosis: In less than three months at the age of fourteen, self-hypnosis, or self-programming, helped me stop stuttering heavily. This technique involves communicating directly to your subconscious. Besides calling it self-hypnosis or self-programming, some call it autosuggestion or auto-programming. It's all about being in a self-induced state of mind for maximum receptivity. It has many additional benefits too.

Hypnosis is an extremely powerful tool because it allows you to go deep into your subconscious and influence its programming at the core of your brain. While it can make for great shows as people under hypnosis do really crazy and funny things, it can also bring out your inner strength like nothing else. In my early teens, I performed hypnosis shows for friends in my basement. Once, while my buddy was in a trance, I suggested that his arm was hard like a bar of metal. Three other friends tried to bend his arm with no success. While my subject looked like he was asleep, he was stronger than we could ever imagine.

In reality, the mind absorbs and accepts suggestions without our logical side filtering them. It's like a complete mental let go and even frees up your imagination. Hypnotherapists are doing wonders for many people with various objectives. They do so by getting rid of fears and phobias, helping them to remember the past in great detail and much more. Hypnosis has proven to be quite effective for helping people quit smoking and other dependencies. It can also greatly alleviate pain. Some even go through invasive surgery without anesthetics while under hypnosis by a professional.

In the 2016 Olympics in Rio, some athletes used visualization reinforced by self-programming. For example, high jump competitors would visualize every move and then replicate them while in a trance. They would do this before their jumps. Now, just imagine if you used this easy technique to reinforce the suggestions that you choose for yourself. All the best advice that inspires you could get in your new preset neuro structure of the brain as you alter it to act differently in the same circumstances. You can change your habits in no time and create your reality as you wish. This is powerful stuff!

Ace #3) Meditation: More and more people are practicing meditation in different forms and intensities. Still, there are many myths and misconceptions about it. Here's a short list of why some people are not convinced:

- *I can't meditate—my mind always wanders.*
- *My mind is used to multitasking. It's not for me*
- *I'm a down-to-earth person. This is for weirdos. It's too "woo-woo" for me.*
- *I don't see myself taking the lotus position, lighting candles—that's not me!*
- *A nap is all I need to reset my brain.*
- *This is wishful thinking. There is no real science to back it up.*

These myths are based on the image you have of monks and yogis dressed in robes and practicing meditation in the lotus position in inspiring settings. Or you see a "New Age weirdo" lighting candles everywhere, with special psychedelic music or images and special energy stones, plus he is filling the room with a special odor. These images of the practice of meditation are not very inviting for most "regular" and "normal" people. But meditation is not about what you wear, how you sit, and even what environment you meditate in.

Ever notice your mind wandering while doing routine chores, like brushing your teeth, washing the dishes, or even driving your car? If so, you're in the alpha zone of frequencies. This means you can meditate during these periods. Have you ever noticed that a long drive sometimes seems to fly by at the snap of your fingers? You were driving in a kind of automatic mode. You were mentally relaxed even though your body was fully active. This means the alpha brain waves are also present during the normal waking state, beta. This mental place between reality and dream is very responsive to suggestions. Personally, I meditate every time I get the chance. When I'm in the shower, or mowing the lawn, it does me great good to refocus and center myself. You can meditate for an hour if you have the time, but just a few minutes can have a substantial positive impact.

Meditation is a simple mental exercise that involves relaxation and emptying your mind of thoughts to then reach and connect to a heightened level of spiritual awareness. The premises for success are very easy:

1. Be comfortable in what you wear and sit, or lie down any way you feel most at ease.
2. Concentrate on your breathing and visualize each thought appearing in your mind, getting further away from it until it has disappeared.
3. As you empty your mind, it gradually relaxes and reaches a state of pure communion with your inner emotions and feelings and connects to your spirituality.

In scientific terms, you reach the frequency levels where you go deeper and deeper in the subconscious mind. The lower brain waves at work are alpha (7.5–12 Hz) for the light meditation and theta (4–7.5 Hz) for deep meditation. Delta (0.5–4 Hz) brain waves have been observed in transcendental meditation, the same brain waves associated with very deep sleep.

For first timers, it doesn't take long to reach the first relaxed state of mind, alpha. Again, alpha is the doorway to your subconscious. Alpha brain waves are just below our normal waking state of consciousness, beta (12–40 Hz). Alpha is where visualization has its strongest influence and the same frequency range as creativity, self-programming, and super learning. We will concentrate our efforts here. When you reach a deep relaxation, you are in a light meditation state.

This exercise aims to get us away from thoughts that get in the way of our true feelings and emotions. Instead of sending suggestions like self-programming, we want to reach a peaceful place in our mind. From this peaceful place you will begin to feel the purity of your feelings of gratitude, compassion, joy, and happiness, and love of yourself and others. A fairly recent discovery demonstrates that our heart emits more electromagnetic frequencies than our brain. More information is transferred from the heart to the brain than from the brain to the heart. Tapping into positive emotions while meditating allows your brain to accept positive vibes that are then engrained in your subconscious and conscious. After time, it becomes a natural state of being. That's the great power of meditation.

Ace #4) Magnetism: Magnetism can be interpreted in many ways. For me, it's not about moving objects with your mind or reading other people's thoughts (telepathy). It's about being sensitive to the energy you emit and the energies you accept. The principles explained in the books *The Law of Attraction* and *The Secret* speak of "asking and you will receive." I agree with this concept, but few truly understand the important premises for it to work. First, if your emotions and thoughts are negative, you will attract negative vibes from others. If you're in a dark place in your mind and heart, you cannot tune in to positive thoughts and inspirations, and you will be connecting to the wrong frequencies of the universe.

A rather recent discovery proves that others can sense this electromagnetic field that radiates from your heart and can even influence their mood. Scientists at the HeartMath Institute have conducted research on the human heart and the energy it produces. The electrical field generated by the heart, measured by an electrocardiogram (ECG), is sixty times greater than the amplitude of what our brain emits, as measured by an electroencephalogram (EEG). These fascinating studies have also found that this energy radiates outside our body and is picked up by others from a distance. The science of the heart electromagnetic field has evolved tremendously in the past few years, and more scientists are studying this energy field we all produce.

According to our feelings and emotions, we can also observe that this electromagnetic field changes. Emotions often lead to the most important decisions in our lives. Just think of the last time you trusted your gut. Picking a husband or wife, choosing your friends, finding a profession, and following your passions are all emotionally driven. For example, studies by Joel Pearson, professor of psychology at the University of New South Wales in Australia, have revealed that for the most important decisions in our lives, following our instinct produces better results than following our logic and reason. Researchers actually found a way to measure how intuition can guide our decisions: by adding negative or positive subliminal images to a test of instinctive decision making. The subliminal images did in fact influence the results. When shown the positive subliminal images, participants were more accurate at their task. And negative images had the reverse affect. They also concluded that the more you practice being connected with your intuition while in a positive mindset, the more adept you become at trusting your sixth sense. Over time, your success in decision making will improve. So our objective is to be tuned in to positive emotions and trust our gut, especially when it feels so right but makes no logical sense.

After college, my logic steered me to continue school and attend university. I studied business there. But my gut told me to immediately join our small family business. My brother and sister, who were five and seven years older than me, had already joined my father's enterprise. We had eight stores at the time, named Panda (they specialized in children's footwear), in the province of Quebec. All my friends and colleagues at school told me how crazy I was and that I would regret sacrificing my education for working in a small business. A close friend even told me I would call him "mister" someday. I was struggling with a choice: Do I follow logic or intuition? Well, against the advice of many, I followed my intuition and as a result, I managed to build a successful franchise chain across Canada by the time I was in my early twenties. I learned more about business than all my friends with a bachelor degree, and this enabled me to become financially independent in my mid-thirties. It was if I had been inexplicably attracted to this real-world opportunity. It was truly magnetic.

Looking back, I can recall many occasions that I let my instinct win over common sense and things always turned out great. I can also remember a few times where I let my negative emotions, such as anger, take over, and that made me do or say things I've later regretted. The same can be true for you. Learning to be more in tune with your own inner positive energy helps you be more in tune with the positive energies surrounding you. Spreading positive vibes will exponentially return the same. Magnetism is all about creating and tapping into positive energy.

This capacity to tap into your intuition requires a kind of mental let go, where you allow yourself not to think and just follow your instincts. It's already happening more often than you think, you're just not always aware of it. You will be able to recognize these "miracles" more and more, in all sizes and shapes.

So there you have it. **The four hidden aces: visualization, self-hypnosis (self-programming), meditation,** and **magnetism.** Each one has enormous power to influence your mindset, and by learning how to use them they will really change your life. Here's the greatest thing about these techniques: They are all do-it-yourself methods. Imagine taking control of your destiny by understanding how you can shape your reality simply by shifting your mindset and creating the perfect alignment from your conscious, subconscious, and even your heart and soul.

Again, we will see how they can work together to achieve any goal. They all offer many benefits for different types of challenges. We will tackle all negativity by using a combination of these powerful tools. You will be able to put into action the "new improved you" by using any tool at any time, because they are always at your disposal.

It doesn't stop there! We will also demonstrate other simple ways to support and reinforce the **four aces** with what I call my **wild cards**—music, laughter, kindness, physical activity, and more. This means that you will be equipped with the complete mindset toolbox, giving you the ultimate power over your mind and spirit.

No More Excuses!

The 3R Approach for Success

To this point, we have discussed reshaping your reality the way you want it to be. We have put forth the notion that happiness and success are choices. Finding excuses for anything can be something of the past. After learning how easy it can be when you see things in a different perspective, you will shift your mindset from the *"I can't"* into *"I can, but won't."* The last excuse remaining will be "voluntary ignorance," and that choice belongs to you.

Have you noticed that many people are great at always finding the "perfect excuse"? They can tell you the best reasons not to do something. They find plenty of support not to be happy, not to be successful, not to have good relationships, and not to have a good day. If we're honest with ourselves, we are all guilty of finding the perfect excuse for some of our failures. Blaming circumstances or others for not having the perfect life is a kind of programmed response, inspired by the attitude of many.

Our reliance on others to solve our problems is also a good excuse to justify our failures. To take things under your control, you must accept full accountability for what happens to you. First, place the absolute responsibility on yourself. Then you need to find a path to your own solutions. Then we will understand how our own ignorance has misled us, and we will get the facts straight about the endless possibilities of human growth. We will tackle the negative sources that have a strong influence in the wrong direction. With the right suggestions and methods to reinforce positive messages and energy, we can build what I call **invincible self-esteem**. From there, you'll find a mindset that will allow you to tap into your best in all circumstances.

An excuse is something that can turn into a challenge in an instant. It's all in your mind, therefore your choice. Conquering challenges is how we grow. Not knowing what will be revealed in the following chapter will be your last excuse!

You will be amazed about your true potential by understanding how to use your mind to create your dream life, your reality. Self-empowerment is a concept that has evolved in many directions and is now supported by evidence and scientifically proven facts. It is explained and demonstrated like never before by my unique **3R approach**. This includes:

1. **Recognize.** This consists of recognizing your inner potential and providing a series of positive suggestions to be inspired by and to use in your next steps.
2. **Reset.** Reset is the process of learning all the techniques to reset your mindset to the core.
3. **Reinvent for Success.** Here you will reinvent your reality through concrete actions.

After each of these, a simple-to-follow action plan will enable you to create new habits in no time and to repeat the process at will. My 3R for success approach will be used first to tackle all negative thoughts and emotions about you and your true potential. You will develop the instinct of turning the negative forces into positive outcomes. The next phase will be to reinforce and strengthen your inner force to better perform in relationships, career, and reaching your goals and dreams while enjoying every moment of your journey and your life.

Now we have established that we create our own destiny, happiness, and success with our mindset. We also understand that scientific evidence supports the benefits of the practices proposed in this work. We are ready to begin the journey of positive transformation. So have fun while expanding your mind and spirit to new possibilities! Keep your mind open to ideas that may seem contradictory to what you have been previously told. Most importantly, enjoy the immediate results during each step of this awesome adventure toward reaching your ultimate goals.

CHAPTER 2

Recognize
Expand Your Mind—Debunk Your Limiting Beliefs

Our Minds Have Been Hacked

As demonstrated in the previous chapter, the power of suggestion works to our advantage when we decide what we suggest to our mind's deeper layers. Also recognize **the great influence of suggestions** from others. Each time you are exposed to a negative thought or emotion, your mind registers it somewhere. Sometimes your conscious picks it up, but many times it goes deeper into the subconscious, even affecting your thoughts, mood, and self-esteem. You register all types of information, good or bad, and that information is then stored somewhere in your mind. In the long run, if a message is repeated often, and over a long time, you start believing it, even if it's the most destructive and false information.

You can expand your mind to reach a positive mindset in all circumstances. For that to happen, you must first acknowledge two very important facts. First, recognize that we have received a tremendous amount of false information that we believe. Second, most of this information has been rather negative. This chapter is about understanding the power of different influences in your life. As we become aware, our conscious can tackle the problem by preparing a series of positive suggestions to break free from all negative sources.

To different degrees, we are all victims of negative mind hacking from many sources. Credible sources like your parents, teachers, doctors, and friends all implant ideas and have a strong influence on your overall perspective, even if what they say is inaccurate. Think of every time someone you respect told you something negative. Maybe they made comments that forced you to question your dreams and goals or your capabilities and possibilities. Quite frightening, isn't it?

As a young stutterer, many people commented about my limitations. They often looked at me with a certain discomfort or pity. This affected my self-esteem. Even my father, who loved me dearly, informed me that I should forget about working in a public setting because I would not be "respected" as a stutterer. He also told me that he read from a credible source that stutterers stutter for life, so I should find my path in a career involving minimal human interaction. Think about that for a second. How could you not believe the statements of a man you deeply love and admire? You'd likely think he has only the best of intentions in mind.

But it doesn't stop there. We can then add to this the negative messages created by generations of social, religious, gender, and racial prejudice, which explains our preset perception of people—the "unconscious bias." On a deep level, this also affects your own perception about yourself. Society has somehow indicated to people of a different color, gender, or social status that there should be limits to their dreams. Social profiling is the result of years of false prejudice. It's almost in our DNA, and we all do it at different levels without being aware of it or having a bad intent. For example, when adults see a little girl, they will compliment her beauty, her pretty hair, and her great-looking clothes and accessories. These all pertain to how she looks. Our comments also send a subconscious message about her identity and what's expected of her. But we don't talk to little boys like we talk to little girls. This type of programming is greatly influential in how we perceive ourselves through the eyes of others. As we are programmed to judge based on color, gender, and more, we are also judged based on irrelevant information. This judgment is often very subtle, but we sense it. The strength of reprogramming yourself is amazing. It can counter years of bad programming that negatively affected your self-esteem. With proper introspection, you get to know your true self more than anybody else could, and that's what you must focus on.

Marketing tries to influence our behaviors with many tricks such as subliminal images hidden in an ice cube or decor or even making you believe you should belong to a lifestyle proposed by a particular product. Have you noticed advertisements no longer discuss the features of a product or the distinct advantages and benefits of any service anymore? It's all about the image of the brand, as if you become "hot and seductive" to those you want to seduce thanks to this little pill or that piece of clothing. The packaging is now more important than the content.

Advertisers make you think you will finally feel happy and fulfilled by wearing a certain brand and logo, or that you will at last love yourself after losing a few pounds, or have better parties and more fun with the best crowd if you drink a specific brand of beer. Marketing strategies are meant to influence your thoughts by connecting to your emotions and sense of belonging. Their promise goes beyond the product itself. It's about relieving a "pain" that sometimes doesn't even exist. For example, marketers will tell you that not having the latest version of your smartphone is like being outdated and not trendy, even if you use your present device nowhere close to its maximum capacity and that it serves you quite well.

Mind hacking can also come from sources you might not even consider or expect. The ideas implanted in our minds by something as nonthreatening as movies influence us. Think of all the movies that paint the picture of good fighting bad with little or no nuance. The repeated suggestions of one side representing the bad is all bad and the other side representing the good is all good have conditioned our minds to often think like that. We can observe this tendency in politics where one side is convinced that the other side is always wrong and vice versa. Nobody is perfect, and nobody is all good or all bad. One bad mistake in your life doesn't make you a bad person. Training your mind to see the better side of people and things makes you live every experience and encounter in a positive mindset. This attitude will lift you and others. Creating positive outcomes instead of negative vibes that give no chance for anything positive to emerge is a conscious choice that you need to exercise every day. With the right tools to reprogram you subconscious, it can quickly become a habit.

Mind hacking can be quite strong. In response, we have to counteract this dangerous and often unintended practice. We create a positive reality through positive core thinking. Many people talk about focusing on the positive. Few have really explained how the power of negativity can be damaging. Recognizing its presence and destructive impact is crucial to beginning to counter these unintended consequences.

The Massive Devastation of Negativity

If you pay attention, you will notice that most people, including yourself, tend to let the negative prevail too often. We are so used to hearing complaints of all sorts that it has become almost a natural reaction. We all know more than one person who seems to attract the negative, and he or she constantly complains about everything! And the endless negative loop continues. This vicious cycle is far too common. If you're honest about it, how many times have you sabotaged a whole day or a potentially great evening for some rather insignificant negative event?

Politicians use the power of negative advertising and fear because they work. The negative messages about their opponents have a greater impact than making those positive arguments about themselves. Even when proven to be false, allegations stay in voters' minds and eventually influence their votes.

If we observe what's happening on a global scale, we can see that a very small minority of extremists are having a huge negative impact around the world. A few people carrying hateful messages and actions have created chaos everywhere. This negative energy feeds prejudice and ignorance, and the cycle of hatred and violence escalates out of control. The majority of good people are undermined by a very small percentage of radical and violent extremists. Then the manifestation of violent behaviors is more likely to occur when one is exposed to violence in some form or another for a prolonged period. The cycle of violence from being a victim of abuse to becoming an abuser is well documented. Sadly, this pattern is far too common and is practically impossible to break if you don't reprogram all levels of your mind, including your emotions and your spirit.

Another demonstration of the great influence and power of negative energies is the devastation post-traumatic stress disorder (PTSD) causes. A traumatizing experience can have damaging repercussions lasting for years, even for a lifetime. The pain runs so deep that it affects every part of your being. You can be marked forever by just one instance of trauma. Notice the difference between people coming back from war compared to people coming back from humanitarian rescue missions. Both have seen horror, but those who participated in rescue missions after a natural catastrophe often come back feeling fulfilled and with hope and belief in humanity. That's because they have seen solidarity and joint efforts to save people in great distress. Those who witnessed war firsthand often return with depression or suffering from PTSD. The destructive force of a strong negative experience is overwhelming and sometimes even too much to bare.

The less extreme negative experience and suggestions also impact us. Carrying negative thoughts or feelings is like carrying a heavy load. It drains your energy. The continual negative programming is the pathway to stress, anxiety, even depression. Some physical illnesses have also been proven to be symptoms of someone's mental state (psychosomatic).

Negative emotions take many forms. These include jealousy, anger, regret, hatred, stress, anxiety, envy, greed, addiction, depression, prejudice, and many more. They all have something in common: If not resolved, their intensity will increase. They can create catastrophic effects, sometimes even resulting in violent behaviors for you and toward others. While the negative emotions are often aimed at another person, you end up paying the price of the negative energy you create. Reacting negatively to someone is like letting him win over you. The ultimate victim of any negative energy you harness is you, your self-esteem, and your state of happiness. How can you expect to perform in any situation when you are filled with negative emotions?

Again, it's all about the mindset you choose to give yourself. This is the choice you must make to reach your dreams and goals. And this is the topic of conversation for the remainder of this book. For example, by being indifferent, you don't give people (or situations) the ability to affect you. Always stay above these challenges and never let them control you. Easier said than done you may think, but you will soon recognize that it's not that difficult when you learn to create positive suggestions and make sure these messages are anchored deep in your mind and soul.

Our efforts will begin with easy visualization images that will equip you to discard the negative thoughts and emotions that are preventing you from being truly happy and fulfilled. From that strong base, you will start building **invincible**

self-esteem by recognizing your true potential. You will understand that *self-esteem is not about your current situation, it's all about your true unlimited potential* and what you decide to do with it.

Maximize Your Potential, Reach Beyond "Set Limits"

Great news! It is possible, even easier than you think, to switch from a negative attitude and perspective to a positive one. Simply take concrete steps outlined in this book and make them part of your life. Remember to recognize that entertaining negative thoughts is a choice and an excuse for not being happy. Positive thinking is a mindset that anyone can choose.

Numerous and very powerful rewards emerge from focusing only on the positive. Making every moment and relationship precious is a true life-changing experience, never to be ruined by negativity. Life is a great adventure. We are all confronted with many challenges, small and big. The most horrible events you may encounter must never stop you from dreaming and moving forward. You are still alive, and that's worth trying to make the best of! If you really look for it, there is much beauty in many people and places where we forget to notice. No matter what happens, even in the most horrible situation, you get to decide how you will deal with it and the actions you will take. No one has control over what you think, believe, and dream. The ultimate goal is that positive thinking is at the root of your belief, regardless of any negative situation or event.

There is also a great opportunity for **global positive change**, as outlined in my first book *The Big Bang Project: Creating Humanity's Best-Case Scenario*. All iterations of the future seem bleak, dark, and negative. My mission is to seek positive possibilities for our future generations. Society is made up of individuals, and we are improving society by empowering individuals. This is the "from a better me to a better we, and from a better we to a better me" cycle I referred to earlier. So from self-empowerment, to local commitment, leading to global impact is the best route for positive change to happen on a global scale. The beauty is that *what you can do for your country" is also about what you can do to better yourself*. Everybody wins!

The **recognize** phase is about being aware of the positive and negative forces that influence your life. Then you can focus on recognizing the key factors of success.

With that said, here are the first exercises I want you to do:
Exercise 1: *Identify what and who is bothering you.* Make a list of the sources of your stress, anger, frustration, fear, deception, or any other negative thought and emotion. For it to work best, trust your intuition as you make this list, don't think! Just brainstorm and let your instinct rule. This list represents your conscious recognition of the negative sources in your life. It is normal to miss out on a few things that affect you in a negative way. Always be mentally aware of your state of mind. Visualize a kind of mental buzzer that emits a beep in your mind every time you have negative thoughts or emotions. As it is virtual, you get to imagine the sound the beep makes; make it unpleasant so you must react to it. This **virtual negative-thought buzzer** will ring less and less as you add items to the list to be dealt with.

Our next effort will consist of getting rid of the possible negative sources that get in the way of your happiness and success. This first step involves resetting your conscious with visual suggestions that will enable you to turn anything negative into a positive outcome. We will then start anchoring these positive images deeper into your subconscious with the right suggestions to reprogram positive thoughts and emotions. From there, you can take full control of the techniques to elevate your mind to the next level and achieve top performance in anything you aim for.

Exercise 2: *Identify the positive elements in your life and what makes you happy.* This list is of great importance. A huge part of countering damaging thoughts and emotions is to learn how to mentally go back to your true passions and recognize who and what makes you really tick. You will rediscover your hidden dreams, and most importantly, the positive emotions associated with what you really love.

This means we will gradually learn the different techniques to be used in achieving success in all the important aspects of our lives: self-esteem, happiness and well-being, relationships, career and wealth, and health. All of this is possible with the right approach. As you program positive suggestions, you also create the mindset required to make it a way of life, a new lifestyle.

As we go along, you will master gradually and effortlessly the easy techniques proposed earlier. Allow your imagination to lead your efforts in reprogramming your mind. As you learn to let go mentally, you learn how to reach the right brain frequencies, and therefore to enter the gateway to the deeper layers of your mind. Most importantly, you must have fun during the whole process. The positive mindset of having fun in getting better is the base of positive change. For example, you may want to lose weight, but the proposed diet and exercises are like a kind of torture. If you feel that way, your efforts won't last very long. Make it fun, always.

Recognizing the Key Factors of Success

The **recognize** phase is crucial in mind reprogramming. It is the conscious mind's responsibility to be aware of our thoughts, emotions, and state of mind. Your conscious must also be in a constant learning mode to seek inspiring suggestions and images to then communicate them to your deeper subconscious and spirit.

The Incredible Power of the Mind

So far we have recognized that our complete mindset is responsible for almost everything in our lives. We understand that we can reprogram our deeper levels of consciousness to create our own reality. We also know that science has evolved so much in different fields of expertise related to the great capacity of our mind and spirit.

Recognize from this point on that YOU have it in you. You are equipped with the same mind potential as anybody else. It's not a question of IQ, it's about using the full potential of your gifts and talents and living your passions. Realize that you are better in many things than a "smarter person" can ever be. It's also about what you do with what you have and how you can enjoy fulfillment in all aspects of your life.

Your mind is managing the brain, the heart, and the soul. Your mind gets to decide how to interpret situations and people. Your mind chooses action versus procrastination. Your mind creates nuances and extrapolates, exceeding your five senses, even the three known dimensions. This incredible power of the mind to anticipate, to react, to make its own interpretations, to learn, to feel, and to have a sense of right and wrong is at your disposal always! Therefore, learning mindset tools is a great opportunity to improve all aspects of your life.

It all starts with visualization. Our next chapter will demonstrate how visualization tricks can turn all negativity into positive thoughts, emotions, and actions. You will learn how to communicate effectively to your subconscious to start the greatest journey of creating your reality the way you really want it to be.

CHAPTER 3

Reset Your Mindset
Where Do We Begin?

Let the transformation begin! In the **reset** phase, you'll learn how to communicate suggestions that will resonate throughout your whole being and replace old negative thoughts and emotions with positive ones. To do so, we will turn to the first of the **four hidden aces: visualization.** First, let's discuss one of its various applications.

Turning Negative into Positive: A Conscious Effort

The conscious mind can identify and choose the best suggestions for the reprogramming process. Then its job is to use the most impactful method(s) to help these positive suggestions sink into our core levels of the mind.

Mental visualization is one of the most powerful tools I have learned and still practice almost every day. Your mind registers images in your conscious and subconscious and repetitively uses them to reinforce retention and execution. With the right techniques, you can achieve anything you set your mind to. Visualization can take many forms for many purposes. Top athletes use this method to constantly reach their highest levels of performance and to always surpass themselves.

We're not all athletes, but like them, we require visualization to perform at our optimum. To that end, I use my imagination mixed with visualization for many things, as it helps me focus and be in the moment. For example, I will sometimes choose my virtual "Cirque du Soleil" hat. When unpleasant winter weather descends and turns into freezing rain, making paths and stairs slippery, I become a pretend artist of Cirque du Soleil, performing a risky number. I'm like an actor playing a role; one trip turns into a great balancing act where every move is calculated to perfection. With the mindset that comes with my virtual hat, my predisposition and concentration levels are at their peak. Without this extra focus, I would have probably broken my neck more than once!

To build my confidence while I programmed my subconscious for public speaking, I would visualize myself on stage talking like a pro and feeling great. The same can be true for you. Always visualize yourself "already there" and enjoying the feeling of being that "new you." Start by simply visualizing doing the things you dream about doing and being happy in the process. Your conscious effort will decide the perfect image to visualize that fits with your specific challenges, dreams, and goals. You will then start to create a new proposed reality for your subconscious.

Later, we will use visualization to reinforce chosen suggestions while in meditation or self-hypnosis. It will be used for self-esteem building, relationships, and to increase your performance at work and play.

Premises for Success

To succeed, your mindset must be in the best zone possible. Reprogramming your subconscious requires that you are calm and relaxed. For visualization to be most effective, take a moment before to prepare your state of mind.

The following recommendations will help you achieve great results even without using meditation and self-hypnosis, which will be discussed in the next chapter. As you learn to relax your mind, you learn to go deeper into a state of total mental let go. Remember, you can practice these visualization tricks just about anywhere and anytime you are performing mundane chores, like brushing your teeth, washing dishes, or while in the shower. You can also use them "in the moment" to better focus and perform. So here we go.

First, start with a few deep breaths to bring your body and mind into a relaxed state. Often, three to five deep breaths is enough. Each breath brings you deeper into your relaxation, and you feel your mind more and more void of stress. Many yoga teachers will teach that breathing starts with exhaling, not inhaling. Have you noticed that in normal breathing, when you exhale, there is still air left in the lungs? For the first two breaths, try to expulse this air reserve with an extra effort of pushing it out. Imagine at the same time that you are purifying your lungs and thoughts with every breath of fresh air. Imagine that every time you exhale you expulse negative thoughts and every time you inhale you receive calming and comforting thoughts.

Now that you are relaxed and ready to visualize your goals, use the following images to turn negative thoughts and

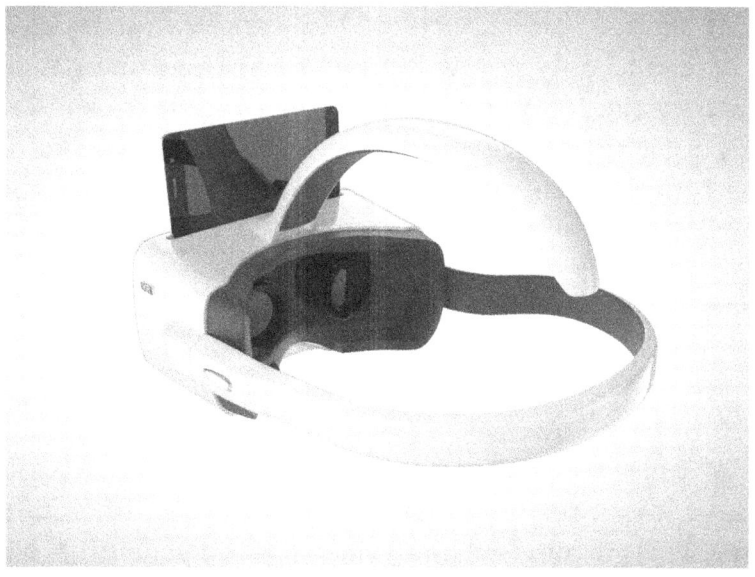

emotions into positive and productive outcomes. To begin, imagine you are wearing your ultra-comfortable **super virtual mindset helmet**. It comes with these great features: tinted glasses (in your favorite color) with the option of virtual scenery (beach, mountains, rivers . . .) and headsets playing your favorite calming music.

It also comes with a very practical virtual warning; the **virtual negative-thought buzzer**. Every time you entertain a negative thought or emotion you believed you had discarded, you imagine it rings. Choose a virtual unpleasant and loud sound that will make you react immediately. To turn it off, offset the negative by its positive counterpart (the other side of the coin) or simply an unrelated positive thought.

There's also a special **balcony view** feature that enables you to observe as a spectator. When you take a step back, you become more "neutral," which allows you to analyze the situation with a more open mind. Having a global perspective instead of a misdirected negative narrow focus gives you the possibility to notice more positive points of view. Remember that like everything else, the more you practice, the better you become. By the way, remember that your **super virtual mindset helmet** is, well, virtual! You can wear it anytime and anywhere, and only you will know you're wearing it!

Next, try the following simple visualization tricks that will help you get rid of negativity and see the positive side. Have fun with these ideas. They are designed to be simple and fun and WORK!

Getting the Negative Out for Good: Five Easy Visualization Tricks

Identify and scale

Some people seem preoccupied, worried, and anxious or stressed without really knowing why. It is very difficult to turn negative vibes around when the cause is too general. A list will

help you find the best arguments and positive messages and images to overcome the source of negativity. Try to create that list before you begin with your relaxation and visualization. When you look back at it with a relaxed state of mind, you can then revise your list using the **balcony view** option.

Your first list may not contain everything that's bothering you. In fact, you may even forget about an important issue. When you remember these challenges, you can simply add them to your list. This list will change on a regular basis, as you remove the **discarded problems,** and think of new ones. Revise your list on a regular basis (at least once a month) so you can re-evaluate every item on it.

Beware of the packaging. Just like gift boxes, sometimes the more valuable or heavier gifts are in the smaller packages. The first negative source on your list may also not be the most important. Imagine that you scan the negative elements one by one like at the supermarket. Instead of a price, it rates the importance level on a scale of 1 to 10. A green light will appear for the scores between 1 and 3. Don't waste your precious time for insignificant problems. Get rid of these **insignificant** problems by being **indifferent.** Recognize that you mustn't let "meaningless" people or events win you over. They don't have the merit to take some of your precious time and energy directed at them. Imagine now that you put these thoughts in the **discard section**. Create your perfect image of getting rid of these insignificant people or situations for good. Imagine a blackboard where your problems are written and you erase them one by one. You may also imagine a garbage disposal mechanism or that they disappear into space or at the bottom of the sea. Choose a personalized image that works for you.

These small problems can really add up. If you let them affect you, even in a small way, the sum of these insignificant issues can become quite heavy. Concentrate your energy on problems that drain you the most. Every small or big negative element that you free yourself from gives you more energy to tackle bigger problems. If once discarded a negative thought comes back, then you must hear your **virtual negative-thought buzzer** and remember why you discarded it. If the thought comes back and back, maybe you underestimated its importance. So go through the next steps until it is ripe for discarding for good.

A yellow light will show for the problems rated 4 to 7, and a red light for the more important negative sources, rated 8 to 10. Follow exercises with a few yellow problems to get the hang of it. Your confidence will build by achieving success with smaller challenges, and then confronting the bigger challenges will be easier.

Clear your mind with a few deep breaths, and begin the next visual exercise.

Wheel of Perception

The lottery spinning wheel or "wheel of fortune" is my favorite image, and I use it often. In this exercise, you will visualize your own version of this wheel. It is divided into two sides: a red side, which represents all negative interpretations, and a green side for the positive arguments. The

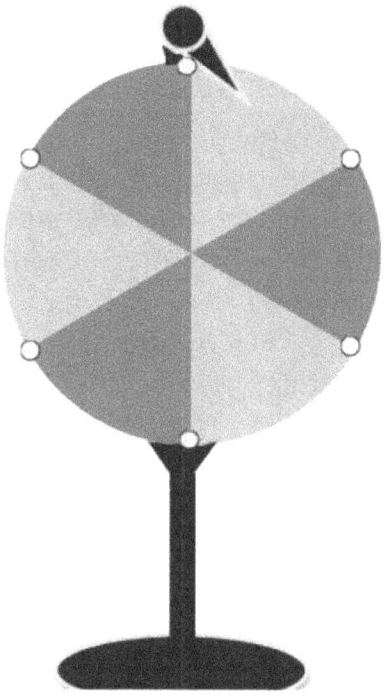

advantage of a virtual image on this wheel: You get to turn it with your mind. This exercise helps you see and focus on the positive. You will notice many positive arguments, then you can choose the most convincing for that specific issue. The **balcony view** option is often needed for this exercise. You need to take a step back to better see all the positive possibilities.

Here's an example that demonstrates it's all about how you choose to see things. This is the story of a boxer who had a long career. He held what was considered to be a very unenviable record. Although he had a great winning record, he was knocked to the mat often. When being interviewed, he was asked how it felt to carry a reputation for getting knocked down more than any other boxer in the history of boxing. He simply replied with a smile and said, "This is the thing I am the proudest of, because it means I'm the boxer who got back up on my feet to win the most often!"

They say there are two sides to every coin. Always try seeing the positive side. Again, the more you practice, the more it becomes natural and instinctive. Realize that every negative source is a challenge you can overcome so that you can ultimately grow every time you are confronted by any challenge.

To this point, you should have discarded some of the negative issues impacting your life. But for those that remain, follow the next visualization trick:

Relatively speaking . . .

This is where you compare and are inspired. When I complained about anything as a child, my parents reminded me to compare my situation with those in poor countries living in far worse conditions. They shared with me that many of these children didn't even have food or water. Their argument was quite convincing. After hearing it, I felt pretty stupid complaining about my small issues. Putting your problems in perspective by looking at them from a less fortunate person's point of view should make you realize how privileged you really are! Acknowledge all that you should be grateful about. As you dig, you'll likely notice that list can be quite long.

However, I find the opposite approach even more effective. Rather than contrasting the good with the bad, how about *being inspired by the best?* Many inspiring stories can change your outlook. These might be stories of incredible people defying the odds to overcome insurmountable challenges. Look for stories where people were in your situation or even worse. There are plenty of them around, and you can easily find them through social media or the Internet. They are proof that when you really set your mind to it, there are no limits! Transpose these examples of greatness and make them your images of your own future. This exercise of associating an image with inspiring ideas will help you not only remember them better, but more importantly, retain them better and faster with a greater layer of consciousness. When you revise an image in your mind, as mentioned earlier, you can also feel it. Your emotions are allowed, even encouraged, to take part in the reprogramming process, as long as they remain positive.

Understand that life is simply a contrast in perspectives and there are always people experiencing more difficult challenges than you. Again, this visualization will most likely help you get rid of just about every negative thought, simply because you have acknowledged and visualized the best possible outcome through real life examples.

Time travel

Time travel offers you two options: to visit your past or to imagine your future self. Revisiting the past as a spectator enables you to go to the source of some events that marked you. As mentioned earlier, finding the sources of the problems is not the most productive approach. We will try to focus on the source of our inner strength. Our brain has this incredible capacity to revisit our memory and see from a certain distance. Have you noticed that when you recall an event, you don't see it always the way your eyes saw it? Your mind has extrapolated all the information from all the angles it perceived and observed and created a kind of movie for you to visualize.

Now, try to go back to the most positive events you can remember, moments when you were happy and proud of yourself. Frame shot your greatest memories in your mind—times when you performed your best. Use these moments as references to your capabilities. When faced with any challenge, use these positive memories to find your inner strength.

You can also time travel to your past to remember your childhood dreams and passions. You may discover a new path from your old dreams. All accomplishments are the results of a vision. Visions of a better future are the starting points to create them. Imagine a happier version of your older self. What makes you so fulfilled? My father often told me that you must remember that every day is an opportunity to create a great memory for your future and a chance to build a better tomorrow. This means that today is potentially better than yesterday and probably worse than tomorrow, *because one day in life should always make a difference.*

Another question you want to ask your older and wiser self is, "How important and significant will my present problem be part of or affect my best possible future?" The answer will most likely make you see that you attach too much importance to a temporary challenge, and that you can and will resolve it.

What if your spirit just took a "time-out" from your "avatar"?

The image above may seem strange at first, but it suggests a very powerful message. Sometimes we all feel we are living in a kind of cruise control. We tend to carry negative past events as weights under our wings. It's almost like our true spirit is somewhere hidden underneath this huge pile of responsibilities, stress, regrets, and all the everyday distractions.

Try for a moment to imagine that your spirit is just appearing in your body. Try to imagine that your body is the avatar of your soul and essence and your spirit wants to have fun and make the best of this gift that is being able to enjoy physical experiences. Imagine how your soul would be amazed by all the possibilities. Your spirit would **totally disregard the past, or what you don't have, and would focus on the NOW and what you have!** I often try to imagine what could be my soul's perspective on things. This allows me to admire and be grateful for this life on a regular basis. People who have experienced "life after death" after a near-death trauma all come back with a new outlook. Their new perspective always translates into a life-changing experience; they understand better that every moment is precious, and they become dedicated to their purpose and true mission in this life.

I'm very confident that these visualization tricks will help you exercise your mind to think positively. But even then, you'll still recognize obstacles and challenges that may test your willpower and fortitude. That is just part of life. However, when the going gets tough, we can collectively work to reset our self-esteem so we can better handle these challenges.

The next chapter is about reprogramming your subconscious by speaking directly at it with the techniques of **self-hypnosis** (**self-programming**) and **meditation.** These methods will allow you to reinforce your chosen suggestions from images and words that have marked you positively. Use them to program your mind to the core with anything you wish. That's the power of your subconscious: It's very malleable. You can convince it to believe what you want it to believe. So before we move forward, let's recap this chapter and keep the most convincing arguments that you'll want to communicate deeper into your consciousness.

We have established that the conscious mind has the responsibility and the power to reprogram by recognizing the best information and creating positive images and suggestions. We have learned the power of imagination and visualization to turn negative thoughts and feelings into positive ones. We can create many different virtual hats to get into the zone, such as the **super virtual mindset helmet.** We are now equipped with a **virtual negative-thought buzzer,** always ready to react when entertaining negative thoughts and emotions. We can always use the **balcony view** feature to take a step back and re-evaluate. We are ready to communicate at a deeper level by entering the **gateway** to your deeper levels of consciousness.

Relax and enjoy. This is going to be easier than you think!

CHAPTER 4

Digging Deeper to Reset
How to Speak and Influence the Subconscious

Now you will begin to learn and exercise reprogramming at the source. The techniques presented include the **four aces: self-hypnosis, meditation, magnetism,** and **visualization**. While visualization was covered in the last chapter, in this chapter you will learn how it can be integrated into many topics as a powerful support. You will learn how to choose and give the right suggestions to your subconscious, using a combination of visualization and the other techniques. At all times, you will carry these four aces. This mindset of having a virtual winning hand of cards will allow you to control any situation like never before. Imagine carrying this important advantage in your mind, always sure of yourself and capabilities. This virtual poker hand means you are always in charge of your thoughts, emotions, and your life. You own the mental advantage!

The four powerful mind-programming techniques of **self-hypnosis, meditation, magnetism,** and **visualization** will help you mold your thoughts, be in the moment, perform your best in any challenge, and remain in tune with your inner peace and pure positive emotions. Then you will master the law of attraction by learning how to connect and harness positive energy from yourself, others, and the universe. To complete the five-card poker hand analogy, I will then propose other mindset tools you can use for many purposes—my **wild cards**. Four aces and wild cards win every time!

The great force of these techniques is that they are **self-managed, self-executed,** and **self-monitored**. This is **self-empowerment** in its purest form. You, and only you, will control every stage while influencing yourself with your choice of words and images. *You become the absolute mastermind of your destiny by creating your new reality.*

Power Programming by Self-Hypnosis

At the age of fourteen, my mother gave me the best gift I ever received: a book on self-hypnosis. I don't quite remember the title, something like *Helping Yourself with Self-Hypnosis* or *The Power of Suggestion*. It was in French, my first language. It absolutely changed everything for me. In three months, I learned to conquer my worst fear for good. I went from being a very heavy stutterer who was constantly afraid to speak in public, to a DJ who loved speaking before crowds without ever stuttering. I've used self-hypnosis ever since for many purposes, and it sparked my interest to learn more and more about our mind and how to create and enjoy my dream life. Our capacity to reach into our inner strength is remarkable and should be enjoyed by everyone.

This self-empowerment tool of self-hypnosis is extremely powerful and has practically no limits. It is easy, accessible, takes little time, and procures many benefits. First, understand the power of the subconscious. It is like the master program of a very powerful computer. Like a sponge, it stores all information from all sources. It's malleable, believes what it is told, and can be reprogrammed with any new suggestions. It is safe in the sense that it cannot be programmed to do what your profound self would not, unlike a computer. That's why, for example, there are limits to what a hypnotist can have people do, on stage or in real life. Our instinct of survival and deep values are part of the core subconscious programming and act as a safeguard.

The subconscious is very active during your sleeping hours and when you are relaxed. Brain wave frequencies are lower and your imagination is at its peak. The gateway to suggestions is registered in the alpha frequencies, just below the normal waking state, beta. Your conscious is still active while influencing your responsive subconscious.

Forget about the excuse that you can't find the time. A daily fifteen-minute séance will give you so much more energy and focus. This translates into saving a lot more than fifteen minutes in efficiency and productivity. When I'm busiest, I take more self-programming breaks. They enable me to perform better for a longer time.

Let's get started by learning how to get in the mental zone for reaching straight to your subconscious. Again, it's all about relaxing your body and mind for a perfect set-up.

Time of day: The perfect time to take is simply your perfect time. This means you can choose what works best for you. The easiest times are when you are going to sleep or when you just woke up in the morning. These moments are already close to the brain waves related to your subconscious, because you just slept or are just about to. At night, some people feel they fall asleep quicker. Without you realizing it, your subconscious registers all your suggestions and carries them into the deeper layers of your subconscious while you sleep. In the morning, you will benefit from the extra energy and focus while continuing to reprogram yourself. The first times you try, you may want to choose these periods. But when you're at ease with getting in the proper relaxed state, you can practice self-hypnosis just about anywhere, anytime.

The night sessions are recommended for getting rid of deep-anchored issues, such as habits and fears. It is the best time to tackle the more general life goals or when you would like to ask a specific question of your subconscious.

The day sessions are designed to reenergize you, refocus you, and help you get rid of the accumulated stress of the moment or the day. Only three to five minutes will suffice. For example, you can take just a few minutes when you come home from work. You recharge your energy by eliminating the fatigue and stress of the day. This way you better enjoy the precious moments the evening has to offer.

Create a daily routine where you get used to doing it at a certain time. But you can break that routine anytime you wish if you are persistent and find at least a few minutes in a day. Sometimes an emergency session might be needed, like before an important business meeting, or a job interview, or a romantic encounter that makes you nervous.

Duration: This is entirely up to you. As alluded to earlier, only a few minutes can do you much good. A fifteen-minute séance is extremely beneficial and highly recommended when addressing more important or deeper issues. Not only will you have reprogrammed your subconscious in a great way, you will have received the equivalent of three hours of sleep. For me, a lifetime insomniac, this is very precious. You will be amazed if you trust your inner clock. Set a duration in your mind before you begin, and you will wake up exactly when you "asked" your subconscious to.

Body position: Lying down or sitting, both positions are good. At first, you will probably find it easier to relax by lying down—it's more natural. You want your legs well relaxed with your feet a little distanced, aligned with your waist. Your arms must also be totally relaxed. If you are sitting, armrests are recommended. If there are none, simply rest your hands on your thighs. When lying down, put your hands a couple inches away from your body. Your fingers facing the mattress enables your fingers and shoulders to be more relaxed. It's all about allowing your body to completely let go and making sure your circulation flows freely. So be very comfortable. Try also to wear comfortable loose clothing. If you are sitting, take your shoes off if you can.

Environment: Soft music will help induce relaxation. Some prefer no music. Again, it's very personal and up to you. For starters, the surroundings must be calm—your bedroom, living room or office, or outside where it is peaceful. Note that while in a trance, if the phone rings, for example, it won't bother you. After getting used to it, you can practice it just about anywhere. When you become more accustomed, you can take a moment even at crowded places. For example, those that have experienced being hypnotized on stage say that their conscious knew what was happening but acted as a spectator, watching but not really controlling. This means the subconscious mind can "be in charge" even when confronted with many potential distractions, like being on stage before a laughing crowd.

Breathing: This is the key element. Each breath counts and is associated with images and suggestions to get you in a trance, meaning that your alpha brain waves are fully active. Breathing properly is how you get completely relaxed.

Self-hypnosis has two phases. The first one, preceding the actual self-hypnosis phase, is about getting relaxed. Start by concentrating only on your breathing. Take deep, controlled breaths. Remember, a complete exhale is the secret to a complete inhale. You also want to use abdominal breathing for a more profound and consistent breathing. Instead of having only the thoracic cage move, your abdomen should go up and down too. The thorax will also go up a little after the abdomen is full, and that's normal. This breathing technique is well known to singers, actors, and orators. It is part of their training to better control their breathing and stay calm during their performance.

In this first phase, clear your mind while breathing. Try this little exercise: Take twenty deep breaths in a row without any distractions in your mind. Sounds easy? You will notice that some distracting thoughts tend to appear. This is normal. Most people get at least a little distracted after seven or eight seconds. When this happens, start back from zero and continue. You will feel more and more relaxed as your distraction-free count improves. You don't really need to reach twenty straight before you step into the next phase. After only a few minutes, you are ready for the body countdown.

The **body countdown** is a countdown that helps you use each breath to become more and more relaxed. This is an example of how it goes, once the first phase of breathing is completed:

You imagine you feel the strength of gravity pulling you down and this feeling of being heavy increasing with each breath, to a point where you feel you cannot move. Start with your extremities, arms or legs. The order is not important. Personally, I start with my toes and work my way up my legs, but many start with their fingers, up to their arms. Again, do what feels best for you. Get your whole body completely relaxed. Feel your body heat increase and circulation flowing in your veins—that's how relaxed you want to be. Here's a rather detailed example:

> *First breath.* I feel my toes of my right foot getting completely relaxed and heavy.
> *Next breath.* I feel my right foot getting completely relaxed and heavy, as my toes continue to get heavier with each breath.
> *Next breath.* I feel my right calf getting completely relaxed and heavy . . . as my foot and toes are warm and heavy . . . so much I feel like I can't move them.
> *Next breath.* My right thigh . . . you get the picture.

Then you do the same for the left leg. After both legs are done, move on to one arm and then the other. Start from your fingers, then move to your wrist, your forearm, your bicep, and finish with your shoulder. Always imagine and feel all the parts already visualized, completely relaxed with each breath.

After the shoulders, focus on your neck then your facial muscles. Once done, make a final countdown starting at ten. Each breath brings your mind and your whole body to total relaxation, deeper and deeper. Use your imagination to create the perfect picture of getting to zero. For some, the picture shows them gradually going down weightless toward the bottom of the sea, where it's totally peaceful. Some will prefer seeing themselves floating weightless into the clouds. In your imagination, you can breathe under water and anywhere your heart desires. At the end of the countdown, you know you are ready to propose any suggestion to your subconscious. You are exactly in the zone of maximum receptivity of your inner sponge, deep in the alpha brain wave frequencies. If you want to test your receptivity, although it's optional, you may want to try the following fun exercises.

Testing the trance. There are many ways to confirm that you are in the right mental state. Let me propose three exercises designed to test the trance. The first one consists of imagining a balloon gently tied to your wrist, and this balloon is gradually filling up with helium. When it's full, imagine your arm slowly lifting, completely without effort. Now, as you imagine it, your arm actually rises, like magic, without you consciously asking your muscles to move. Then, when your arm is halfway up, the balloon is pierced and your arm slowly goes back down by itself. If it worked, your trance is confirmed.

You can also try the heat test. Imagine there is a source of heat, like a fireplace, close to your feet. As the heat slowly rises, you feel the heat stronger and stronger in your feet. But at some point, the intensity of the heat is almost discomforting. Then the heat source dies down, and you feel your feet cool gradually to the point of total comfort. If you truly felt your feet getting warm, then hot, then warm again, you are right in the perfect mental zone, ready to move on.

Another way to test your trance is the technique of "ocular blockage." You'll see what I mean. Imagine a count from one to ten. Each breath and count makes your eyelids heavier and heavier. At ten, you can't open your eyes. They are glued shut. If you are incapable of opening your eyes, bravo! It worked.

You are now officially in the perfect self-hypnosis state. Let the power programming begin!

Choice of images and words. There is a good way, and a wrong way, to speak to your subconscious. Let me explain the bad way first. The subconscious has a funny way of remembering things. It will not remember the negation of a word or image. For example, if you state in your suggestion "I am not afraid of . . . ," your brain will register "afraid" and will completely ignore the "not." So you are accentuating the word you must avoid at all times: afraid. Your subconscious accepts any negative proposal. This is very important to remember, and it's a great exercise to word things properly and positively.

Learning to see yourself succeed instead of fearing failure makes all the difference. One focuses on positive, therefore creating the positive scenarios. The other focuses and attracts the negativity that you are programming yourself to receive. Always hope and visualize the best outcome before and during any situation, encounter, and challenge. Elite athletes visualize every move many times over and remember only their best performances as a reference. Roger Federer once said that the ability to quickly forget bad performances is crucial to succeeding.

When I learned self-hypnosis to get rid of my very heavy stutter, I pushed the idea in my subconscious that I was great at speaking and that I loved it. I made all my suggestions and visualization images based on success. I always avoided the word "stutter" in my list of positive suggestions. Instead of seeing myself like a stutterer who is trying to stop stuttering, I pictured myself already as a great speaker, at ease in front of people. That's why it worked and took so little time, even at the age of fourteen. That's also why when I talk about it, I can disassociate myself from the stutterer I used to be and absolutely love speaking in public and sharing my experience.

As demonstrated with my visualization tricks, the conscious mind plays an important role in the reprogramming process. The subconscious prefers hearing short, powerful phrases, where each word becomes filled with meaning. Repeating short sentences with key words is your goal. The right choice of words can make all the difference in reprogramming your subconscious. This means you must always be on the lookout for inspiring messages to integrate them into your list of powerful suggestions and turn them into short, powerful phrases. It is therefore recommended to renew your mental images once in a while to complement and strengthen your intended message with a fresh perspective. These suggestions can then be regularly prioritized to be used later in your self-hypnosis sessions.

As demonstrated, words and images are very powerful. Combined, the impact becomes almost exponential. So you want to try, when possible, to associate a key phrase with an image and an image with each phrase.

The other key factor of success when speaking to your subconscious is repetition, repetition, repetition! When you really want any skill to "sink in," the more you repeat the exercise, the faster and better you reach your goal. It's like anything else—practice makes perfect. This means you should find lesser but stronger images. It is better to repeat in your mind many times the same thing than imagine many different things only a few times. The more you visualize a certain behavior or action, the easier it becomes to do it. Many studies have shown that visualizing an action many times over is equivalent to doing it many times over.

Perseverance is truly rewarded when it means building a habit of seeing the positive side and discarding the negative side. Your brain's neuro pathways will respond and adapt to the reprogramming, and after thirty days or so, ten to fifteen minutes per day, the mindset will become automatic.

Meditation: Connecting with Your Inner Peace

While self-hypnosis helps you communicate specific suggestions to the deeper layers of the mind, meditation is almost the opposite. Its sole purpose is to free your mind completely of thoughts while being as relaxed possible. The objective is to truly be in the moment and connected to your inner peace.

Meditation is well known and has been practiced all over the world for centuries. It has many variations and intensities. Many books have been written on the topic. Now I offer my take. I offer a simple approach to meditation, with a simple goal: to help you connect with your spirituality and feel positive and constructive emotions. The more you practice meditation, the more it becomes instinctive, and it evolves as an intricate part of your being.

The preparation to relax your body and mind suggested earlier is also good to set yourself up for a meditation session. Any way you find to reach total relaxation is good. For meditation, you may not need to do the body countdown, especially for short sessions. You can just concentrate on your breathing and imagine yourself in the most beautiful, peaceful place you would want to be and go there in your imagination. Your subconscious will believe it, because your logic is off.

The duration of your sessions is again up to you. A few minutes will be very beneficial and easier to integrate into your daily routine. That's more important than the duration. If you are a novice, start gradually. Don't push yourself to where it becomes inconvenient or too arduous. Start simple.

You don't have to be in a lotus position to meditate, and you can do it in many situations (where you don't need your complete focus). For example, you can take a moment during your morning shower to empty your thoughts and concentrate on tapping into your positive emotions. Just relax, concentrate on your breathing, and feel grateful to be alive.

Meditation is as simple as that. You reach a deep relaxation, and you fill your heart with humility, gratefulness, joy, love, empathy, fulfillment, self-awareness, and all positive emotions and images of your life. You are in the moment. The present is all that counts. You are free from anxiety about your future and free of the deceptions and frustrations of your past. You let go of your logic and let your heart be the guide.

When you can take a little more time for a séance of meditation, it allows you to reach a more relaxed state of mind. Then you connect with the deeper layers of your subconscious and you also connect with your spiritual self.

Meditate to cherish what you have instead of wishing for what you don't have. Being grateful for your life is also a meditation exercise. Don't get me wrong. I don't mean by that not to have dreams and goals to better your situation and your life. But never forget to enjoy the moment and recognize what you should be thankful for. You can also create a list of reasons to be happy. Writing about what is precious to you helps you realize that you have something positive to build on. When in a trance, focus on that and that alone. Compare your life with a car ride in the most beautiful scenery you can imagine. If you focus on the dead flies on the windshield, you are missing out on the most beautiful things to see along the ride toward your destination.

Be imaginative and always try to ask the right questions. It's not about whether the glass is half-full or half-empty. Rather, ask "Is the liquid left enough for me?" The real quantity in the glass is more important than the size of the glass! A bigger glass half-empty may contain more than a small glass that is full. If you want your glass to be full, just get a smaller glass. If you need more liquid, find a way to get some more and appreciate the value of each drop you have as it becomes more precious!

Meditation should help you find a balance of energy within your life. Yin and yang is also a very old Chinese concept of "the perfect balance of energies." Good comes with the perfect harmony of energies. And bad, or evil, comes from an imbalance of yin and yang. Finding unity in duality is the essence of its symbol. The awesome balance of nature is demonstrated everywhere on earth and in the universe. This law of polarity is what the symbol is all about.

Magnetize to Receive Positive Energy

Your soul and spirit—our pure essence—is energy. This energy flows in every molecule of your body. It is this energy that makes us feel alive. It is channeled everywhere in your body, reaching every corner of your body, mind, and soul. Your brain's neurons communicate by electric pulses. Your heart produces even stronger electromagnetic pulses than the brain. All this energy is also connected to our aura, the energy that goes beyond our body. Your aura connects to other people's auras. When you encounter someone, the union of both your energies becomes a unique energy field made of this temporary merger. Notice if a third party steps in, the energy changes. A large crowd will produce a very different energy than an intimate gathering.

A negative vibe someone gives off can be felt from quite a distance, and instantly. I'm sure you can recall a situation when someone arrived in a room or to a conversation, and suddenly the energy turned around, making everyone feel instantly uncomfortable. To that end, you have to project the type of energy you wish to receive. Remember, what comes around, goes around. This simply means that if you project negativity, you are most likely to receive just the same.

By always projecting positive thoughts and actions, you attract all the positive back. They say that a smile attracts a smile. Well, it's true. Treat people nicely, and you'll be treated with respect and kindness. Ask yourself this: Are people having fun and feeling uplifted in my presence, or are people experiencing a negative moment? How good does it feel being around me?

The law of attraction is rather simple but not always well interpreted. Some will claim that the "secret" is simply to ask and you will receive. As I mentioned earlier in the book, I agree with this only somewhat. There is an important nuance. You can only receive positive energy if you are in a positive energy mode. What you emit is what you attract. If you are in a dark place in your mind and heart, you cannot receive anything but negative vibes.

This is remarkable when you think about it. We are somehow connected in an energetic realm of reality. The science community and spiritual believers are now agreeing: *Space is not empty.* This name which I mentioned earlier, grid of dimensions (GOD), came to me in a vision, where all energies in all dimensions cohabit and are interconnected in the universe in the field (science's name for this area, which I mentioned earlier in the book) and in what religions call God. When you pray, someone is listening. I call upon my "cosmic friends" often, and like magic, miracles of all kinds have happened. You can call your angels or your "God" by any name, at any time, and know that someone, in some other dimension in this energy grid, is there and listening.

This also means that all possible frequencies are part of this grid of dimension. The question becomes this: *What frequencies do you choose to tap into?* Imagine an endless radio tuner and you get to dial the frequencies you feel like connecting with. Countless possibilities, nuances, and intensities exist. The "dark side" and "the good" are both expressed in infinite shades. Being aware of your capacity to decide to dial the positive energies surrounding you enables you to create positive outcomes.

The more you tap into your deeper mind, the more you become in touch with your intuition. Your gut feeling is what you should trust. It comes from an emotional and spiritual place.

Voilà! With these four aces, you are ready to reprogram your mind at the deepest levels, create new habits, target new goals, and finally, create your dream reality. You can start applying and practicing all four techniques right now, today, or tonight. In the following chapters, I will propose different suggestions, ideas, and images for all major spheres of your life. Following that, you will **reinvent** your life through concrete actions.

To this point, we have discussed communicating with your subconscious. Through **self-hypnosis, meditation,** and **magnetism,** you should feel better equipped to reinvent your mind with positive energy to move forward in the direction of your dreams and success. But these techniques do not stand alone and can be supplemented and supported by a slew of resources to ensure success. That being so, the next section will outline **self-empowerment** tools to help you better control and manage your emotions. These can be used to either release the excess stress or anger, or better focus or stay calm and relaxed, or even to induce joy. These techniques are known and practiced by many for the longest time and have proven benefits.

These are the wild cards I mentioned earlier. Though I don't play poker, I love the visual analogy of always carrying a winning virtual hand. The strategy is to create positive vibes and energy any way you want, any time you want.

Wild Cards for a Perfect Hand

My wild cards come in many shapes and sizes, but they all act as support beams in the tremendous house you are building. Use them to support your journey and help you gain clarity in the relationship between your mind and the outside world.

The Power of Music. Music has many great virtues. It makes your brain light up like nothing else. Every region of your brain is touched: nostalgia, emotions, imagination, memory and anticipation, the tempo that makes you tap your feet or dance, your feel-good center, and more. Moreover, it touches your heart and soul. It speaks to your whole being. That explains why we love our artists so much and why they can move us and inspire us in unbelievable ways, just with a song.

Sounds are emitted in a range of frequencies we can hear, and sound frequencies are in tune with our body and soul. Most popular songs are played at about sixty beats per minute, the same as a normal heart rate. That's no coincidence. Notice how the tempo drops for ballads compared to party and dance songs. Whether you want to relax or mentally escape, or you wish to be energized and celebrate, or add more romance, or feel more focused, even euphoric, music is the perfect vehicle to carry you there.

Many people will prefer listening to very soft music to help them relax faster during self-hypnosis and meditation. So try it, and see if it helps you. Some will even induce their relaxation and performance by using binaural beats or other technology that emits specific frequencies to help them reach the desired brain waves.

Some of these new technologies have proven to be quite good. To be honest, I don't really feel I need them. Maybe I would investigate more if I were a top athlete or had a very stressful life or difficulty relaxing and felt I needed additional help. Beginners may also appreciate the assistance for getting in the mental zone quicker and with more ease. Do your research before you choose such a device; that's my best advice.

Primal Scream. This instinctive method of venting fear, anger, and more by a loud scream is used by all of us at one time or another. It's our primal instinct kicking in. When you suddenly hurt yourself, screaming somehow relieves a bit of the pain and you feel better afterward. Physical effort is often enhanced by a kind of scream, like in martial arts or tennis. Some women tennis players, like Maria Sharapova, use this technique, and it's obvious. Many books have been written about the benefits of the primal scream. I am sharing this tool with you for two important reasons: One, it's a great tool that your conscious can use to release the negative and two, help you find your inner warrior. We all have in us this "inner warrior," this primal instinct to defeat great threats. By screaming your own warrior voice out loud, you let out this innate strength. Let this primal instinct out, and find the survivor/warrior in you, and you will feel stronger against any obstacle. Try it, you'll be surprised.

Relearn to Laugh. Laughter is proven to be very beneficial for your mind, body, and soul. Your brain loves to laugh. Laughter produces endorphins and procures a sense of well-being and relaxation. It releases stress and tension. Laughter is also contagious. It lights up a room in no time and creates a kind of bond with those you are laughing with. Only positive things can come out of laughing. Sometimes, I intentionally provoke my thoughts to find something funny I can laugh about, and I'm back in a "feel great" mode. Some people have forgotten how to laugh. It is very sad. Go back to the time travel visualization to remember what used to make you laugh. This mindset can be reproduced at will. It just takes a little practice.

Have you noticed that people who laugh at themselves have great self-esteem? That means they have understood that to err is human. De-dramatizing and not always taking yourself too seriously is an asset in all circumstances. It takes the unfounded pressure out of wanting to be perfect at all times. When you make what you consider to be a stupid mistake, the option of laughing is far better than the option of being mad at yourself, especially when the consequences are relatively not so bad. Again, avoid the negative option using every means at your disposal, and laughter is a great choice physically and mentally.

A Healthy Lifestyle. That's no secret to anyone. Physical activity is great for releasing stress, fatigue, anger, and more. Your body reacts by discharging endorphins, which produce a great sensation of calm and pleasure. This is one of the reasons some people get very intense and are almost hooked to their sport. They love the high it produces. A punching bag is better than a victim. Release your accumulated stress and anger in a positive way. Run, swim, dance, workout, or enjoy any sport you like. Find an activity you can love. You will eat better, feel better, be more alert, and more able to relax.

Self-empowerment also means that you choose what you eat. Many healthy recipes exist. Find a variety of choices that you love. This book is not a cookbook for self-empowerment, but of course it is part of the journey for a more successful **reset** and a complete mindset for success. Your capacity to relax is far greater when your body is well fed.

The Magic of Kindness. Being good to others is a great gesture for you. Kindness can take many forms, like a smile, a hug, a listening ear, a simple gesture like opening a door for someone or giving your seat on the subway. Many have discovered the virtue of giving. For one thing, it's probably the best "feel good" sentiment of all. They have also realized they are helping themselves just as much as they are helping others. I have much to say on this subject because I believe it makes all the difference; if you want maximum positivity for yourself, giving to others is essential. It has become the norm for many of the most successful people. They use their power and influence for good causes to take matters into their own hands, and most are great philanthropists.

Once you find balance between the internal (your body and mind) and the external (the world around you), you can turn to better pursue your ultimate goals and passions. What are your passions? How often do you practice them? How passionate are you in what you do? These three simple questions are too often neglected, yet are so important in the quest for happiness and fulfillment. Make a list of your passions. Prioritize the ones that are accessible to you. Include them in your new routine. For example, while I watch my daily portion of news on TV, I take this opportunity to play guitar too. To make it easy, my guitars sit next to where I watch TV. Here's another example: I am not very passionate about going to the gym and lifting weights, but I want to stay in good shape. So I stay healthy by practicing things I love doing, like playing tennis, ping-pong, badminton, and swimming. When you love doing something, it is much easier to find the time and the motivation to pursue and persevere.

You get to decide what your passions are. They are yours and yours alone. Nothing and no one can take that away from you. When you practice something you love, you suddenly feel the moment, forget your troubles, and even evacuate the stress. As you learn to dig deeper into your emotions, you may discover old passions that you forgot. Sometimes your intuition can guide you. When you reach a mental let go, you can be surprised at what comes out.

I surprised myself while studying for my MBA in 2005. A teacher asked my class, "What are your three biggest passions?" We all felt a little off guard. That's not a question we got asked often. While everybody struggled to find three things they were really passionate about, I was trying to prioritize my long list of tennis, guitar, reading, traveling, and on and on. My turn to answer came up, and I responded spontaneously. I simply said, "Life, people, and the moment." The teacher said that in her fifteen years of asking this question of all her classes, she had never heard this answer before.

Eleven years later, a monk I met during my travels asked me this same question, though with a small twist: He asked me to reveal my top five passions. I responded instinctively almost the same thing as eleven years before: "Life, family, people, the moment, and fulfilling my life's purpose." He also had never heard this kind of answer before and seemed amazed at how it came out naturally. I understood then the reason and why I'm so happy all the time and why I love being around people and why I'm so driven to fulfill my life's purpose.

This introspection was quite revelatory for me, in the sense that this mindset, built with years of positive thinking, allowed me to love life at every moment, to find a way to appreciate every encounter, even through challenges. My intuitions and passions strengthened my belief in my life's mission and ultimately influenced my journey toward knowing how to get there. Take a step back and find your passions and your path; they are already inside you. The answers will magically come when your mind is relaxed and stress and anxiety free. When you get in this mental state, everything you ask for will be revealed. That's my "secret."

Now that you know all the ways to mold your thoughts and emotions, the **reset** is well in motion. The following chapter will propose ideas to build your **invincible self-esteem** by helping you learn to love yourself unconditionally. It all starts by loving and believing in yourself. This is the foundation for building strong relationships with others. You need to know and believe to your core that you can achieve any goal, any dream.

CHAPTER 5

Recognize and Reset for Complete Success in All Aspects of Life

Now we're going to help you create perfect suggestions and images that will reprogram your mind so you can achieve success in every area. First, we will discuss an overview of each topic, then outline the key factors for success. This list should inspire you to find what sounds right for you, as this is your personal journey. While some suggestions may seem obvious, they will act as subtle reminders to the subconscious and promote growth and further development. *So, open your mind and your heart, and feel within humility, gratitude, happiness, and success!*

The Humble Human Perspective: Recognize Your Greatness

Building an **invincible self-esteem** is like constructing the foundation for positive change in all spheres of your life. It starts with your own perception of yourself, as well as developing your endless potential. You should work to understand your greatness. So let's begin by resetting your self-esteem with a very powerful image that everyone should embrace: the **Humble Human Perspective**. It has the power to change your view of others and yourself.

This perspective is the reason you should always embrace and celebrate YOU. The same qualities that make you unique also make you beautiful. The universe is full of wonders, and you are one of them! We can all gain by knowing the real you. Your current situation is not always the right reference to love yourself or not, but your unlimited potential is. This means you must always value your true potential, even during the darkest chapters of your life.

With all this said, please take a moment to try on my virtual **humble human hat**. One size fits all! As you put it on, it comes with these thoughts:

- *I am humble before the universe, for its immensity is beyond my comprehension. It holds so many mysteries we may never unlock.*
- *I am humble before our galaxy, for it hides countless diverse wonders we have yet to explore and understand.*
- *I am humble before earth, for its incredible diversity, the awesome delicate balance of nature, its great power, and all it provides.*
- *I am humble before mankind, for its great resilience, ingenuity, creativity, and diversity.*
- *I am humble before you, for all the skills, talent, knowledge, and experiences you possess that I don't.*
- *I am humble before my own potential, the life I have, all what I can do and give, and how my ideas, inspirations, and actions can make a great difference.*
- *I am humble before the opportunity of learning from you, to share and contribute with you to make this world a better place.*

You can better appreciate diversity with these thoughts in mind. They comprise the universe, nature, and our individuality. We all complement each other, which is one of our greatest strengths! *So thank you for being different and unique, as you add to the world your distinctive colors and nuances, which we can all benefit from.* I can only grow from the inspirations given by your unique perspective. I need to recognize and embrace that even though I possess unique skills and ideas in many things, many people, from every race, society, gender, and faith, are smarter, stronger, and have more talent than me. And where others are weak, I am strong. Again, the awesome balance of nature is expressed by our incredible diversity.

Perfection is not applicable to humans, so accept your flaws, as they make you human. Be grateful for your strengths and qualities. Notice how you can replace the word "humble" with the word "grateful" in the **Humble Human Perspective**. In doing so, its meaning might change but remain just as strong.

Reset Your Invincible Self-Esteem: Bring on the Bullies

If you can recognize and feel this unconditional respect for others, you also recognize, believe, and feel the unconditional respect you must have for yourself. Judgment is a terrible quality. People who judge often don't feel secure with their own self-esteem. The bullies you encounter are the best example of people who don't feel good about themselves. Their pathetic attempt to undermine you results from ignorance and bad esteem and internal vision. Ultimately, we should not be afraid of them, but rather sad for them. We should in fact pity them, even offer to help them or find help. Most likely, they are victims of lack of love. Do not let their words affect you in any way, as they are wrong. If they don't want help, they don't deserve your attention. Be indifferent, and they will leave you alone and try to find a better victim, one that believes them and is troubled, even scared by them and their insults.

Celebrate your individuality and uniqueness, even if others consider it strange or weird. The counter image of any negative perception based on any type of prejudice is to be proud of your differences. This means as a premise for success, you must leave behind all these negative vibes directed at you and others:

prejudice, scepticism, blind partisanship, ignorance, preconceived notions of superiority or inferiority, and any form of violence, intolerance, or exclusion. So how do you do that? Here is a *list of suggestions and images to reprogram your subconscious to love yourself:*

Relax your mind, take deep breaths, reach "the zone," and power program yourself to love yourself by repeating your preferred suggestions and images in your mind and heart. Here are some of my favorites:

Self-Esteem Power-Programming Suggestions

- "I'm beautiful in many ways. I'm great in many things."
- "I love many people. Many people love me."
- "I love myself and my life."
- "I'm an exceptional human being."
- "I'm proud of who I am."
- "I'm grateful to be me."
- "I can and do accomplish anything I want."
- "I can, I can. I do it, I do it."
- "I love challenges. I grow and better myself every time."
- "I keep on improving every day, and I love it."
- "I'm a good person with great values."
- "I'm a positive contributor to society."
- "I give and receive only positive vibes."
- "I'm great at what I love doing."
- "I love doing what I'm great at."
- "I can bounce back from anything."
- "When I fall, I get right back up."
- "Bring it on, I can handle that and more."
- "I'm proud of the legacy I will leave behind."

Self-Esteem Visualization Ideas

1. See yourself as beautiful, and focus on what makes you beautiful in your unique way. Visualize and feel that long list.

2. Visualize situations where important people in your life love you and are grateful for what you do and who you are.
3. Visualize you being happy doing what you love.
4. Visualize how you make a difference in many people's lives.
5. Visualize yourself as "already there" in any goal you have.
6. Visualize yourself at your best in all circumstances.
7. Visualize yourself happy and successful.
8. Visualize yourself growing from defeat, failures, and losses.
9. Visualize all the things you have that make you happy.
10. Visualize yourself being able to do anything, almost like you had super powers.

Self-esteem is all about your perception of yourself at the deepest levels of your mind. By reprogramming your mind with positive images and suggestions, you begin to rid yourself of all the negative unfounded suggestions from the outside world. Your subconscious will only believe what you tell it to believe. Never forget that.

Reset Your Relationships

Relationships impact every single sphere of your life: love and romance, family, friends, coworkers, clients, bosses, neighbors, contacts, networking, and hobbies. Everything revolves around building positive relationships. While trying to build fruitful relationships, recognize and deal with toxic ones, which drain your energy and are a negative source within your life. Repair or discard these. If you believe in giving a chance to a faulty relationship, try to treat the other person like you would want them to treat you. Do what you would do with a close and precious friend: *Elevate them in your presence, show them respect, and be positive with them. Focus only on the best of what they can offer. Be kind. Be curious and interested about their accomplishments. Show you care.* Start with a positive talk and tell them that you want to better your relationship with them, but it has taken a negative turn and you wish to restore a positive relationship. However, if you feel that you, or this person, is not sincere in giving or receiving kindness, discard and become gradually indifferent to this person. He/she has no positive value in your life if you can't make it better.

When you are aware of the importance of building positive energy in your relationships, you are also more in tune to the intent of other people. You can then react faster in your favor, either by strengthening or eliminating. To that end, let's review a list of some of the most valuable affirmations you can introduce into your life to determine the best kind of relationships for you.

Relationship-Building Power-Programming Suggestions

- "I have fun being around people."
- "Every encounter is precious. I make the best of it."
- "I'm grateful for my friends and family."
- "People are happy around me."
- "I emit and receive only positive vibes."
- "I love many people. Many people love me."
- "I'm at my best with people. People are at their best with me."
- "I surprise people with my positive impact."
- "_____ top three qualities are _____."
- "_____ is a good person. I bring out the best in him/her."
- "_____ will love helping me with _____."

Now let's consider an exercise to help you visualize the positive types of relationships you'd like to introduce into your life.

Relationship-Building Visualization Ideas

1. Visualize your next positive encounter with _____.

2. Visualize _____ being nice to you and you being nice to _____.
3. See yourself having fun with _____.
4. Imagine a positive conversation and outcome with _____.
5. See yourself always at your best around people.

As you reinforce your mind to focus only on the positive that all relationships can bring you, you must also make a conscious effort to act on them. Don't forget to ***magnetize*** your relationships by emitting positive energy. As discussed earlier, the energy you send creates the energy you receive.

Success and Wealth; Recognize and Own the Key Factors of Success

I was born into a family of entrepreneurs. I grew up around all kinds of businesses my father and mother owned. These included restaurants and retail stores, a small local airport, my mom selling nylons and other products from our basement, and my father's many entrepreneurial ventures. I consider myself fortunate to have earned my MBA after I had already had many years of business experience and success, which gave me a different perspective compared to the younger students in the course who had to rely only on theory.

My wife still owns a Panda retail franchise; that's how I met her in the late nineties—I fell in love with my franchisee. I now own a coaching/mentoring firm, real estate properties, and multiplexes. These all allow me to have time for my family and personal passions. I've enjoyed this lifestyle since the age of thirty-five, in 2000. I don't say that to brag. Rather, I'm just setting the table for my approach to wealth and freedom. First off, I'm far from being superrich. I'm nowhere near the famous 1 percent. But my most precious asset is the time I spend with my loved ones. It's all about making your life a success, not your bank account and material possessions.

Consider what you want to really be happy. Ask yourself this: "How much is enough?" Success is really having the perfect balance of wealth and the time to enjoy it. I may have sacrificed making even more money when I "retired" young, as many were quick to point out. But the trade-off is that I am always there for my kids and wife, living my dream life, which is not that luxurious and expensive, but priceless. The point is that what makes you happy doesn't necessarily come with an expensive price tag. My house is not a mansion, but it's by the lake and big enough. I don't often go to expensive restaurants, but my wife and I love to cook great meals together. My car is not a Ferrari, but it's fast enough. My boat is not a million-dollar yacht, but it's perfect for waterskiing.

Don't let your quest for financial wealth be your only quest for success. Most things that make you truly happy and fulfilled have to do with enjoying life with people you love. Too many people have sacrificed their most important assets (people they love) for more wealth and power . . . and regretted it later. That said, one of the best ways to find balance is to build a lean and smart company. If you do so, you will find it easier to balance your time at work with your personal time.

The business management experience and knowledge I have gained through the years helped me understand how to make businesses of all sizes prosper. Creating the perfect environment for success for a small or large corporation is very much transposable to personal financial achievement.

The first element to succeeding in any job, career, or business is to be passionate about what you do. Understand your important role in the lives of your clients. If, for example, you're a garbage man, visualize that you are really the "clean-up guy" of people's garbage. The name "garbage man" does not reflect your contribution. You don't create the garbage, you get rid of our garbage for us. I used to tell my salespeople that they are not just selling shoes for kids, they are also assuring proper growth in a perfectly fitted shoe and that's super precious for the kids' parents. Plus, they are making sure the children are wearing comfortable shoes they love. They understood that they were much more than just shoe salesclerks—they were an important part of children's lives and moms' peace of mind too. Make a list of your positive contributions to your clients. Again, positive reinforcement is the key to reprogramming your conscious, subconscious, and your whole being.

In many ways, having a job is like having a business. **Imagine yourself as the top-level management of an incredible business: your career.** Even if you are an employee, you sell your trade, and your boss is a kind of customer who is willing to pay for your services, know-how, and skills. That means that if you see yourself as the CEO of a top brand (YOU), you understand that the quality of your work and your attitude are your reputation in the trade that you're in. That's what you need to build on to get better jobs at better conditions and to succeed in any business venture.

Here's my top twenty list of the most important **key factors of success** for any business I speak at or where I mentor:

1. Have a clear vision and mission; let everyone know what you're all about.
2. Have the perfect business plan; know where you're going in every detail.
3. Identify and know your clients.
4. Build the perfect team and the perfect organizational chart.
5. Be a leader: inspire, motivate, support, and mobilize.
6. Learn everything about your trade (macro and micro) and your competition. Identify the opportunities, threats, and challenges, and your strengths and weaknesses.

Benchmark regularly with the trade, the best in your industry, and your best.
7. Build on your distinctive skills, own your niche, become the "reference."
8. Learn the best means and the best messages to communicate to your clientele.
9. Create the best shopping experience—the "wow factor" and "360-degree approach." Aim for consistency.
10. Identify, measure, monitor, and prioritize your key factors of success and profitability. Know your key performance ratios, as numbers don't lie.
11. Create and encourage the best possible flow of information, from you to your team, between colleagues, from the team to you, and from you to your customers and them to you.
12. Continually improve. Be proactive by being ahead in knowledge and information—the cycle of the 3R approach for business (**recognize, reset, reinvent**).
13. Be efficient. This is the ultimate approach for maximum productivity.
14. Manage growth and efficiency while keeping your head above the clouds.
15. Leverage your equity and increase your income. Cash flow is about building and leveraging your financial equity and all your assets (your team, clients, know-how, expertise, brand, and reputation).
16. Network and radiate beyond your base clientele.
17. Build positive relationships with your precious extended team; every supplier, service provider, and outside help are your allies and part of your strength.
18. Have fun and create a pleasant and positive environment for you and your team. Always keep the passion alive.
19. Managing is about identifying the right questions, then finding the right experts to arrive at the right answers. No one is an expert on everything. Learn from the best.

20. Respect and share always your company's (and your) values and code of ethics.

These topics sum up the most important steps to creating the best conditions for success. They are taken from my business education (school and mentors) and life experiences. They are meant to inspire you to visualize each issue in your own career or business venture. If you respect these principles, the likelihood of success increases exponentially. Now, let's work to make them part of your life.

Here is a list of suggestions and images to use during self-programming. By repeating these power phrases and visualization exercises while in the right state of mind, your subconscious will believe them. Your mind will take these suggestions as the new core programming at all levels.

Success-Building Power-Programming Suggestions

- "I'm proud of my work."
- "I feel great knowing I help my client(s)."
- "I am reaching the next step in my career."
- "I have success in everything I do."
- "I love teamwork. We all pull each other up."
- "I will close the deal (or get my raise), because I work hard and they need me."
- "I provide priceless benefits to my client(s)."
- "Every day I'm getting closer to having my dream (house, car, job . . .)."
- "I know what I'm worth, and I prove it with my skills and good work."
- "I love what I do, and I'm great at it."
- "I love what I do, and it shows."
- "My boss (associates) notice my passion and are proud of my contribution."

Success-Building Visualization Ideas:

1. Visualize your next goal happening soon and with success, and create and repeat the perfect scenario in your mind.
2. Visualize clearly what you want next to happen, and see yourself already there.
3. Visualize yourself already enjoying the things you want.
4. See yourself living your dream lifestyle.
5. Picture your clients being wowed by your service.
6. Visualize your boss and colleagues loving working with you.
7. See yourself connecting greatly with important people.
8. Visualize the perfect scenario of your next important meeting or job interview.
9. See yourself as the person who can achieve anything and get what he or she wants.

Success is truly determined by your mindset. There are no ifs, maybes, or buts. It's all about recognizing the **key factors of success** and then owning them to your core. Then, by using your new suggestions to reprogram your mind and heart, you can believe that you are meant for success. The rest comes with actions that your mind has been programmed to execute. It becomes second nature after perseverance.

Reset Your Mindset and Lifestyle

Work and life balance is important to your overall success, but it is even more crucial to your overall health. Health is about adopting a healthy lifestyle that's custom made for you. Once you have recognized the best foods you will enjoy and your favorite activity to keep you fit, the next move is to create this new habit in your mind. As mentioned earlier, in less than thirty days, these new habits will be natural and effortless. You'll love them so much, you won't be able to imagine stopping them. Project yourself already in shape and healthy, and create the reality in your whole being.

The mind energizes the body, but the body also energizes the mind. So by regularly remaining active, you energize your mind as well. Mind and body work in symbiosis.

Use these following suggestions to reinforce and convince your subconscious that you are healthy and loving this lifestyle. Remember that you are always encouraged to find your own mental images and **power phrases**.

Health-Building Power-Programming Suggestions

- "I eat well and feel great."
- "I am young and healthy."
- "I love my healthy lifestyle, and it loves me."
- "I feel great. I look great."
- "I'm getting fitter every day."
- "I'm numb to pain. I feel great."
- "I love my fruits and vegetables. They make me feel awesome."

Health-Building Visualization Ideas

1. Visualize yourself healthy and loving practicing your favorite physical activity.
2. Visualize yourself older, healthy, and active.
3. See yourself enjoying eating healthy.
4. Visualize the positive energy flowing in your whole body.
5. See yourself loving getting results.
6. See yourself loving and enjoying your new healthy lifestyle.
7. Visualize yourself already cured and disease free.

Understand that *avoiding bad habits for thirty consecutive days will have rewired your neuro pathways the same way as when you create new habits.* By resisting to make a certain action, and persisting, your "craving" disappears naturally over time. So just hang on. It's a matter of days when you use your **virtual negative-thought buzzer** anytime the craving hits. Then you take a few deep breaths and visualize all the benefits of quitting, and reprogram yourself.

Magnetize for Health and Well-being

Meditation and magnetism are related in many ways. Masters in meditation, like monks and yogis, have been practicing various techniques to realign their physical and spiritual energy. Reiki, for example, is a form of meditation that is specialized in energy healing. The seven chakras, identified by masters in meditation, are the energy centers in our body for different spheres of well-being. Just so you know, even though it is not the intent of this work to go deep into meditation training, the list of chakras shown below demonstrate that the link with energy has been recognized for a very long time in cultures and religions from the Orient.

The Seven Chakras:

1. *The Root—Your Power Base.* Located at the base of your spine. It is associated with feeling safe, secure, and well grounded.
2. *Sacral—Emotions, Creativity, Self-Expression, and Sexuality.* The sacral is situated about two inches below your belly button.
3. *Solar Plexus—Confidence and Personal Power.* Located just above your belly button, it is associated with motivation and ambition.
4. *Heart—Love and Relationships.* Right at the center of your chest.
5. *Throat—Communication and Personal Truth.* In the center of your neck, it is the energy point for speaking your truth and asking what you want.
6. *Third Eye—Intuition and Psychic Sense.* Located between your eyebrows, it is associated with your intuition, inspiration, and clear visions.
7. *Crown—Your Connection with the Divine, Universe, and Soul.* This energy center is about two inches above the top of your head. It represents spiritual energy.

You don't have to be a master in meditation to appreciate the benefits of focusing on your inner energy that flows freely in your body, mind, and spirit. As you relax deeper and deeper, visualize these energy centers being filled with light.

Reset Your Inner Peace and Fulfillment

Personal health isn't just a combination of what you eat and how much you move. Wellness, which consists of your inner peace and fulfillment, plays a remarkably important role within your overall health as well. By meditating regularly, you will gradually connect more and more, and finally instinctively, to positive thoughts, emotions, and energy at all times. Your goal should be to enjoy the "now" and focus on what's precious to you. Focus only on the positive vibes, as negativity will drive you off course.

Connecting to your inner soul will bring you the answers you seek. You will feel the positive energy in the form of pure emotions such as gratitude, love, humility, respect, joy, and fulfillment. Let your heart be the leader. Its energy will influence your brain, your body, your deep emotions, and your soul. Connect only with the positive energies surrounding you, from people and the universe.

Self-hypnosis and visualization will certainly help greatly strengthen your efforts to own these positive feelings and thoughts. To that end, consider the following suggestions:

Well-Being Building Power-Programming Suggestions

- "I'm grateful, honored, and privileged to be alive."
- "I'm humble before my life."
- "Every day is magical. Every moment is precious."
- "Tomorrow begins the greatest chapter of my life."
- "I'm grateful and honored to love and be loved."
- "My life is an extraordinary journey. I can't wait to see what tomorrow brings."
- "I love myself and my life."
- "I keep improving every day."
- "I know my life's purpose, and I'm realizing it."

To execute these programming suggestions, consider the following:

Well-Being Building Visualization Ideas

1. Picture yourself enjoying every precious moment.
2. Visualize your spirit entering your avatar for the first time and enjoying this great body to the fullest.

3. Visualize yourself attracting only positive energy from people and the universe (your cosmic friends).
4. See yourself radiate positivity.
5. Visualize all negativity being washed out instantly from your body, mind, and spirit.
6. Visualize the list of all the precious people you love.
7. Visualize yourself being in the most beautiful and peaceful place you can imagine.
8. Visualize your "super powers" to turn anything negative into positive.

Inner peace, well-being, happiness, and fulfillment represent the ultimate quest for happiness in all aspects of your life. Enjoying life to the fullest comes from connecting yourself with the moment. Every moment is part of your life's journey. Don't waste them with irrelevant negative thoughts. Repeat the suggestions and images that resonate the most in your heart. Again, even if obvious, your subconscious needs to hear and visualize what it may have forgotten due to repetitive outside negative suggestions.

Confront Your Demons

Some negative thoughts and emotions can deeply disturb your life. They can directly impact your ability to reset your relationships, your health, your wellness, and of course, your happiness. A deeply programmed negative emotion will be constantly present in your mind if you don't do anything about it. Phobias, fears, and traumas come in a multitude of shapes and intensity.

The solution: Replace these destructive thoughts and emotions that came from a horrifying experience or great fear with their positive counterparts. First off, remember that through it all you are still alive. The past can't be changed, but you can reprogram your mind to focus and enjoy the present and your future. You may have made a costly mistake, but always remember that to err is human and your intention now is to be a positive force by sharing and helping others. That's far better than hurting yourself, or worse, being dead.

I always say that my greatest luck was to confront and conquer a huge challenge at a very young age. From that point on, I felt like I could overcome anything, all thanks to that first triumph.

To win over more serious issues, you also need to trust that you can. And believe me, you can! Just allow more time for your self-hypnosis and meditation sessions. Do more than one session per day. Visualize many times over yourself being cured. Be aware of each time you entertain negative thoughts, fear, or anxiety. Switch on your **virtual negative-thought buzzer** and put it on "sensitive mode." With perseverance, you will win.

For fears and phobias, you can have your subconscious believe anything you want, even to love what you presently hate or fear the most. My worst fear—speaking in public—is now, as I have mentioned, one of my greatest passions. That shift occurred in just a few months. You can achieve a similar shift. Just convince your mind, and confront your fears head on.

Use the best ideas and suggestions from this chapter to create your own path to success. See yourself as the conqueror. Visualize yourself already the victor and stronger every time. You now possess all the tools to mold your thoughts and emotions at will to create the reality you truly desire. You just have to get the hang of it by practicing every day, even if just for a few minutes. It will grow on you as you observe and enjoy immediate results and long-lasting benefits. In no time, you will trust your capabilities. You will feel empowered like never before. This feeling will grow stronger as you persist.

Our next chapter discusses putting all you've learned to good use by taking action. To really be who you want to be, you must do it. You now know, believe, and feel that you can. The rest will come more naturally each day you program yourself and each time you move forward.

CHAPTER 6

Reinvent

Concrete Actions for Concrete Results

What Now?

Don't miss the starting gun of the next great chapter of your life. It begins NOW, in your mind and in your real life. Your actions throughout your life define you. You have the possibility to forge your dream life thanks to your capacity to tap into your boundless inner strength. You now understand the depth of your true potential. You also know that all layers of your mind will believe whatever you decide. You know as well that your thoughts and emotions control your actions. This extraordinary gift must be put to good use. Like we say in tennis, "The ball's in your court."

What do you do with it?

My parents positively influenced me with their values, a willingness to help those around them, and their guidance in business and personal endeavors. My father would often say, "One step at a time son, and make sure it's in the right direction." And my mother asked me often, "What will you do with it?," meaning that when you discover a skill, a passion, a talent, expertise, or know-how, or anything positive you have to offer, you have a responsibility to share it with as many people as you can.

Whenever someone asked my dad how he was, he'd always respond in the same way: "Better than yesterday, worse than tomorrow!"—meaning that every day is a precious opportunity to build your best souvenirs of tomorrow and enjoy the present while constructing your dream life.

So let me offer you my best advice to **reinvent through action** to be happy, successful, and fulfilled. Here is my short list:

- Find and exercise your passions to the fullest.
- Every challenge is an opportunity to overcome and grow.
- Always have dreams—they nourish the soul (dream big, do big).
- Always trust your capabilities. You know you can, and you will.
- Be the best you can with everyone in everything you do.
- Channel the positive and only the positive. Discard all negative vibes.
- Always wear the **humble human hat**.
- Every moment and encounter is so precious, so take the maximum of what they have to offer.
- You become aware to all signs of small and big miracles happening every day, everywhere.
- Realize it's a privilege to be alive. Every physical sense can only be experienced through a physical body. Having a physical body is the exception, understanding the endlessness of your soul! SO ENJOY IT!
- Recognize that when you project positive energy through kindness, you receive all the positive in return.
- Understand that you can make a difference and be part of the solution.

Let me add to this short list a few important key factors of success when it comes to reinventing through action. The path toward your dream life must be planned and then treated with a code of conduct. The following ideas are meant to start your actionable strategy with the right mindset:

Key Factors of Success

Be fully accountable. The first secret is rather simple, but it makes all the difference. We often tell ourselves "I can't," when the reality is that we mean, "I won't." You must take responsibility for your choices. "I can't" says that you have no control over the situation. "I won't" involves a decision or a choice. You stop being a "victim" because you truly understand that you are the only one accountable. You are responsible for your actions in response to any bad event in your life. As you overcome challenges, you start to appreciate that when you put your mind to it, there's truly no limit in the positive possibilities.

Be authentic. Trust yourself and what you're capable of. Be authentic to your values, vision, and what you really represent. Being true to yourself is a proof of self-esteem and embracing your uniqueness. You can't please everyone, and that's okay. You can't win them all, and that's normal. Focus on those that accept and love you for who you are. Never try to be somebody else to please. It won't last if you have to fake it.

Have courage. Courage is being able to step into the ring and face life head-on. The source of the word "courage" comes from the French word *coeur*, meaning heart. There are great books about the topic, and many ways to explain courage. I like to keep it short and simple and use a visual support. So let me sum it up in a few words—*heart and balls* (excuse my French!). This was a slogan in the locker room of the Boston Bruins hockey team, a great rival of the Montreal Canadians. I loved that team because they really represented their slogan. The guys would always give everything they had, every game. Even if they didn't have the best individual players in the league, their hard work and extra effort, heart, balls, and team building made them a team you could never take for granted. Bottom line, a determined person will face the music, give his maximum every moment, get back up after falling, and won't stop until he gets what he wants. That's courage.

It's fun to get out of my comfort zone. Another secret for positive thinking is to enjoy getting out of your comfort zone. Contempt is comfortable, like an old pair of slippers. Having goals and dreams is sometimes a little scary. It requires getting out of your routine, and disturbing it is like risking it. As you try new things, you will have upsets, even nosedives sometimes. But remember that it's always worth it.

What is uncomfortable when you begin becomes easier over time. Then it becomes natural, like a new habit. After thirty days or less, it becomes your new "routine." So try and persevere to ensure your life continually changes for the better. When you realize the advantages of stepping out of your comfort zone, you actually enjoy it. Feed your curiosity, get out of your same old boring routine, and experience new things. This is how we discover passions, new adventures and places, new opportunities, and meet great new people.

Reinventing Your Mind: New Actions Create New Habits

This section aims to help you build a new routine. As you learn to master all the proposed self-empowerment techniques, you'll want to integrate them into your new routine. Gradually, you will find the right timing to practice each on a regular basis. Remember that you dispose of many opportunities to reset your mindset. Short sessions and quick recharge can occur in the shower, washing dishes, lawn mowing, exercising, and in many more activities. Before you go to sleep, practice either power programming or meditation. This will help you fall asleep quicker with a positive mental state to create a more productive sleep. In addition, you will have programmed your mind at the deepest levels.

The mind adapts with new actions you impose in your life, just like new suggestions. Here are the valuable steps to help you make good habits effortless—routine:

Step 1: Make Your Lists

As I suggested, you want to know what's negative in your life and what's positive to be able to act on them. So don't forget to create your lists:

- *The negative sources*
- *The precious positive people and things you already have*
- *Your list of passions*
- *Your goals and dreams (bucket list)*

Have a concrete strategy to tackle each one. Start right by establishing your plan. **Plan, organize, exercise, and control.** This is how you best manage a business and even your life. Further list:

- *Powerful suggestions and images*
- *Things to do to reach each goal*
- *Your target dates*

You are the ultimate decider of your future. If you are serious about making positive changes, you absolutely need to create a clear plan. By asking yourself these basic, but so important questions, while in a state of deep relaxation, the answers that come in your mind are genuine because they come from a place closer to your inner truth. Any transformation begins with an intention and plan. *The next step is to realize your plan.* Being well prepared is also about how to get there. Make it real in your new routine.

Step 2: Establish Your Schedule

Prioritize, and add make-up time for the most important issues you feel you need to address. Go gradually—like with running, you don't start by doing marathons. Make sure you devote time for yourself at least a few minutes every single day. Eventually, these few minutes will become longer and more frequent with no effort, even without you noticing. Your schedule will evolve with you.

Step 3: Do it. Don't Wait.

You win even when you lose. This lesson is huge. You always grow in defeat in every sphere of your life. This is an absolute. If you compare inaction and procrastination with trying and failing, the difference is enormous. Standing still brings you absolutely nowhere. You have learned nothing, you have achieved nothing, and made no contact or networked. The only thing you know is that you didn't fail. This mindset prevents so many people from taking action or reaching their dreams and goals, because they fear failure. They are nostalgic and say, "should have, could have, but didn't" or "always kept it for later, but time went so fast, never got the chance." Don't be that one!

When you lose or fail, you learn what you need to do to get better, learn not to make the same mistakes twice, and therefore, you gain experience, know-how, contacts, and more. You are one, possibly many, steps closer. It is well known that someone going bankrupt after experiencing success will most likely get back on his feet quicker and stronger than before. His failures made him better equipped to succeed in the future.

So stumble forward. Every mistake, every "no" brings you closer to your goal. You build on your victories and your failures. On the opposite end of the spectrum, inaction will create absolutely nothing. No risk, no change, and nothing to gain.

Step 4: Be a Constant Learner

Find the right help, and always invest in you and in what is important to you. You are your most important asset. Think of all the money we invest in other things. Always nourish your thoughts by seeking knowledge from the best possible sources like mentors, coaches, teachers, motivators, speakers, writers, doctors, psychologists, and experts. The most successful people all have these things in common: They read more, research more, and learn from others the most. This form of humility is the ultimate sign of a great person.

Step 5: Monitor Your Results and Progress

The lists described earlier will evolve and change with time. At least once a month, make sure you update your priorities in all areas of your life. It is natural to seek new dreams and new challenges as we advance. The **3R approach** (**recognize, reset,** and **reinvent**) is about constant **renewal, requestioning, self-introspection**, and continual **betterment.**

Like any good coach and leader, you must regularly measure your progress. I strongly suggest you make the following lists to measure your evolution in each sphere of your life. Start by establishing a rating system—1 to 10, for example—of your present satisfaction level in each area of your life: work or school, wealth, overall happiness and well-being, relationships, romance, health and lifestyle, and exercising your passions.

Your bucket list is precious. It represents your biggest dreams. Don't miss out on any. You will regret it. *So make them happen!* Make a list of all the things you want to see, the places you want to go, and the dreams you want to accomplish. Put a target date for everything on that list. Visualize yourself realizing every goal and dream at the moment you predicted. Rate the probability of realizing each goal. You will notice it increases every month as you evolve in your reprogramming.

Monitor your improvement every month by reviewing your new satisfaction level for each sphere of your life.

Knowing where you are, where you want to go, and how well you are getting there is crucial in order to improve.

Next, I want to share with you what mindset coaches for elite athletes teach their protégés. These visualization techniques will enhance your performance in everything you do, even when you are under great pressure.

Peak Performance Secrets to Be Your Best

Elite athletes represent a great example of mindset control. They have to create the absolute best setting in their mind for success under enormous pressure, competing with the best in the world, and they must peak at the perfect time. Self-empowerment at the highest level requires extra discipline and on a regular basis applying visualization and suggestion methods while in a hypnotic trance.

Performance mindset coaches assist many of the top elite athletes. They understand that this edge of mindset control can make all the difference. I thought it important to share with you what we teach elite athletes so that you can be empowered to perform at your top level in all aspects of your life.

The following tricks to create the best mindset for top performance and results can easily be transposed in all your activities. They will raise your level of intensity in everything you try to accomplish and want to improve in.

Memory and Focus

The capacity to better retain information is a **key factor of success**. What you learn and consider important information must stay accessible in your memory. The following easy tricks will help you remember, at will, what's important to recall.

Visualization, while in a trance and wide awake while in execution, is the secret for retaining information and performing with focus. With practice, you can remember every important name, number, formula, image, or information. Here are some of the most effective visualizing techniques used by top-level students and athletes:

The "picture snapshot." Take a mental photograph of what you want to remember. Hear the "click," and frame it in gold in your mind. Revisit this picture many times.

The "story" from your imagination. Create a story with your imagination and associate it with what you want to remember. Make up your own setting, your own adventures and participants. The more original it is and from your mind's creation, the better you will remember it.

Associations. Invent any kind of visual or other association to help you remember a name, a number, a place, or an event. Be inventive, associate with anything original you can think of. Let your imagination be in charge. Self-hypnosis is also a great way to go back in your memory and recall with great accuracy events in your life. Hypnosis therapy regularly employs it to help people remember suppressed memories from as far back as early childhood.

Identify, "red flag," repeat, repeat, and repeat. When you know you need to remember something, red flag it in your mind, and repeat it many times while in a trance.

Visit your past. Gradually go back into your past. Use images, music, and odors as a mental reference of the time or period you wish to recall. See the details unfolding in your mind as you regress.

Memory enhancement helps you remember, focus, and perform in anything at which you aim. Let's take your plans and goals and apply peak-performance techniques to raise your chances of achieving them faster and better.

Peak Performance: From Mind to Action

The most important way to get "in the zone," and stay there, is to mentally let go of all your stress and anxiety and completely trust yourself. Trust your training, preparation, skills, and hard work. One of the greatest challenges for any athlete and performer is to avoid "choking." This mindset is created when you are "afraid" of missing. Your mind is focused on the negative possible scenario. This is when you lose your inner confidence and just focus on not making an error. Switching from choking to being in the zone is all about eliminating from your mind the words "missing," "failing," and "fear" (of missing or losing). *Your mind should be conditioned to always focus on the present, the perfect execution, and the outcome.*

The same comparison can be made in everything you do. The mental let go required in performing results from trusting yourself and your preparation. Mental preparation is enhanced dramatically when you reinforce strong positive suggestions and images during your meditation and self-hypnosis sessions. Again, just like addressing a deeper issue, invest more time in your sessions to enjoy the best possible benefits.

Here are a few ways to help you accomplish this:

Visualize Your Best for Success

The more you visualize a certain action, the easier it becomes to do. Many studies have shown that visualizing an action many times over is equivalent to performing the action over. The following example represents the proof of combining action with visualization to perform at your best:

An injured basketball player takes a few minutes every day to visualize shooting hoops, just as he would be doing if not injured. Afterward, the player comes back from injury with greater success in less time. Take this other example that shows the power of visualization to ensure a top performance: Many years ago, an experiment focused on three groups of players who were given different tasks. In the experiment, the first group would only visualize shooting a number of hoops every day for a week, while the second group had to shoot the same number of hoops physically, and the third group did both—visualize and shoot hoops. The results were quite phenomenal and were demonstrated more than once. The first and second group's performances on the court after that week were just about the same. *The third group, which practiced physically and also visualized the same motions, achieved the best results.*

Every action is the result of a thought and intention, so always visualize yourself giving your best performance. To assist you in finding powerful images, here are a few ideas. You want to personalize each mental image and be very precise in all the details. Fit them with your sport or specific challenge. Be extra accurate in your visual references. Details count in precision and focus. When you are in the zone, your higher frequency brain waves are in charge, but your alpha brain waves are also active because you remain calm and Zen even during an intense effort. This means you must visualize each move before and during your competition, exam, interview, or business deal.

Power Visualization for Power Performance

- Frame in gold your best performances in your mind. Replay the movie in details.
- Imagine yourself doing great under pressure, staying calm, and having fun.
- See yourself with the trophy, high score, or victor.
- Visualize yourself switching to the next gear at will, any time it's needed.
- Visualize your **energy reserve tank** always full and ready to boost you.
- When you miss, forget and visualize the perfect "shot" immediately.

- See yourself grow even in defeat. Visualize what you need to improve.
- Visualize yourself playing with the best, having fun, and doing great.
- Have your personal "Eye of the Tiger" performance theme song, and play it in your mind to refocus.

Power Program Yourself for Greatness

Self-hypnosis is very powerful to get the message across. Create your own, and be as specific as you can. Associate an image with each sentence. Try to reserve one long *and* one short session every day. This extra effort will be rewarded with fantastic results.

Power Suggestions for Power Performance

- "I perform my best under pressure."
- "I trust my preparation and my skills. I can relax, let go, and focus."
- "I love my sport (challenge) and what it brings me."
- "I'm always having fun on the court, no matter what happens, win or lose."
- "I love my sport, and I'm great at it."
- "I love winning."
- "I always have another gear when the going gets tough."
- "I get in the zone before and on the court."
- "The more the pressure, the more relaxed and focused I become."
- "I grow in victory and defeat."
- "My **energy reserve tank** is always full and ready when I need more energy."

Any top athlete or elite performer of any discipline will tell you that practice makes perfect. The more you repeat the motions physically, the better you become. For my mindset exercises, my advice is exactly the same: The more you repeat, the better it works, and the more profound is your reprogramming.

When you combine practicing physically and mentally on a regular basis, there are no limits to your improvement. Start putting your goals into action, set the wheel in motion, persevere mentally and physically, and the closer you will be to getting there.

Use everything you have learned in this book to better yourself and enjoy the rewards. Thrive every day to become the best possible you. As you become the person you want to be and have the life you want, try also to become a better human being. The next chapter is about self-empowerment at its ultimate expression. It is when you go beyond your personal needs, beyond "me, myself, and I." You elevate yourself by giving. You grow by being a positive contributor to society. You improve by influencing and leaving a positive imprint on others. You feed on the positive energy you receive from the joy you bring. You are rewarded in your heart and soul when you see the good you do and from the lives you have changed. You learn more by teaching, and you evolve by being part of the solution. You have the power to make things change for the better in your community and more. That's what I call "from self-empowerment to local commitment for global impact."

CHAPTER 7

The Next Level of Self-Empowerment
A Better ME for a Better WE

Our connection is crucial for our sanity and survival. That is a fact. To survive as a race, we need one another. If we unite to build together, instead of destroying one another, we can save ourselves, our precious resources, and our future generations. This chapter discusses what we can accomplish together.

The concept is rather simple. The better your family, friends, neighbors, and community are, the better you will be. And the better you are, the more you can do to contribute, improving us all. That is why social repair is a very important part of **self-empowerment**. **Self-transformation** and **evolution** are the triggers of social evolution. To that end, what follows is a description of **self-empowerment** and **individual** and **social well-being**.

Leveraging OUR Possibilities:
The 3R for Social Repair

I often find myself wondering how a truly evolved society would function. We all agree that humans have a lot of work to do to get there! We have so many aberrations for a supposedly evolved species: widespread poverty, political and religious wars, deep divisions that are increasingly polarized, human exploitation in all its forms, the presence of corruption at just about every level of government and more, and the waste of valuable resources (natural and human), just to name a few. The list is too exhaustive to completely enumerate, but we all agree that there is much to be ashamed of! Who can really be proud of mankind's present state of evolution?

Aren't we too smart as individuals to act so stupid as a collective?

It's time that we **RECOGNIZE** our failures to better express our evolution so that we can reprogram ourselves as a society to understand that individually, we can make a difference.

It's time that we **RESET** our social behaviors and reprogram our world based on respect and other values we all share.

It's time to **REINVENT** our actions to better reflect our true evolution, values, and priorities to ensure we do not make the same mistakes of the past.

We can enter a phase where the best of mankind prevails—not a utopian concept of an unobtainable ideal world, but a possible tangent of a future closer to our dreams and true potential. This is a great era—it is ours! We are all responsible for the next generations. Let's be remembered as **the generation** that brought hope!

Socially and individually, how we handle diversity is our biggest obstacle and our most important failure. We are trying to evolve to acceptance and tolerance, which really means that we more or less disapprove, but we'll live with it.

Any type of diversity, might it be racial, social status, religious, political, minorities, and sexual orientation, just to name a few, have been the source of tension, mistrust, prejudice, ignorance, and judgment. Diversity has been an important pretext for many wars for so many years. We should instead fast-forward our evolution to *appreciating and embracing the difference!*

You can shift from a negative approach to positive by wearing the **humble human hat** anytime, anywhere. But this time, wear it with a global perspective. The interpretation wheel will then turn to curiosity, wanting more information and knowledge, understanding the opportunity to benefit from new perspectives.

They say that only fools don't change their minds, so don't be a fool! Accept that you must change, I must change, *and we all must change our perspective on diversity*. Our biases are based on ignorance and fed with unjustified hatred that was passed on. This unconscious bias is part of a negative energy that affects us all. Let's reprogram ourselves as a society by evolving from the inside out. It all starts with you and me—or the collective us.

Magnetizing the Energy of Kindness to Reset Globally

There are angels here on earth, in flesh and blood—extraordinary individuals who have devoted most of their lives spreading goodness, love, and generosity. I am very fortunate to have one as a close friend and esteemed colleague. Judith Trustone has spent many years spreading kindness where people think it cannot exist: in prison cells around the globe, including countries in turmoil like Afghanistan and others in the Middle East. Her first book, *Celling America's Soul*, has had a great impact in the incarceration world.

Judith proposes in her book, *The Global Kindness Revolution*, that kindness can change the world. She demonstrates also how kindness is "energy," and that it can be spread among us. She suggests two powerful ways to share and spread this great positive vibe and make it radiate in our collective. They are kindness circles and kindness at noon. You can start practicing these two awesome techniques of **magnetism** today. You will feel it. In your heart and soul, you will sense the positive kindness vibrations you are creating in symbiosis with others. It's truly remarkable.

Kindness Circles

Form a circle and hold hands. Then you all take deep breaths and get your mind free of thought and completely relaxed.

Invite participants to visualize their energy filling the center of the circle. This group energy then connects to earth's energy and the energy of the universe. We let this incredible source of positive energy into our being, and then release it into the universe. WOW!

It's transformative. Everybody feels an inner peace and an energy that elevated them. It's a must experience! This union of energy made us all connect in a very unique way. Sending these positive frequencies out in "the grid" has a positive influence on whom is tuning to the right frequencies, and there are many.

Kindness at Noon

Our planet takes twenty-four hours to complete a daily cycle. What if every hour a large group of people would send out a positive thought, a smile, a kind gesture? This positive energy would radiate in our universe. So, at noon, every day, each time zone would send positive vibrations. Set your alarm on your cell phone to ring at noon every day, and take a moment to call a friend, smile to a stranger, or be kind to someone. Send and receive this universal love. The world will constantly vibrate with the positive energy we all send to it on a continuous endless cycle, repeating itself every hour of every day. That's magnetism on an individual, local, and global scale, all at once! Extremely powerful!

Judith Trustone, even in her late seventies, is continuing to impact the world actively. She has partnered with another extraordinary soul, Atta Arghandiwal. Atta has devoted his efforts to change things for the good in Afghanistan, from helping organize the banking system and trying to stop corruption and division that tears this country apart. He wrote a remarkable book on the topic, *Lost Decency. The Untold Afghan Story*. Atta is an Afghan immigrant in America, and has also been an inspiration for countless other immigrants to better integrate into America. His first book on the topic, *Immigrant Success Planning: A Family Resource Guide*, is a must-read for all immigrants entering a new culture and for all of us to better understand the benefits from their inclusion in our own culture and society. They make up our strength, our diversity.

I am humbled, privileged, and blessed that Judith, Atta, and I are joining forces to create a "spark" for social betterment. You are always welcome to join our ever-growing dream team of positive thinkers and doers for positive change. Sign up at www.thebigbangproject.com, and be part of this movement for global constructive change.

What You Can Do for Your Country Will Also Benefit You

President John F. Kennedy's famous line "Ask yourself not what your country can do for you, but what you can do for your country" inspired a whole nation. But no one, nor any political party, has yet answered this question clearly. Here's my answer to President Kennedy's eye-opening question:

First, as individuals, we are obligated and responsible for positively contributing to the world in our own unique ways.

Second, all the different entities in a community are responsible for making positive contributions to the world. They would benefit from working together for common goals and challenges. Most citizens are part of one of these positive local forces. This means that individuals have the possibility to help and influence their group. Combine these individual efforts with the community's positive forces—that's how the American Dream can really come alive.

Individual Responsibilities

On an individual level, we can take many small actions to make a huge difference. For a country to thrive, it must create an opportunity for all citizens to be part of the solution. Society is comprised of individuals. The better we are as individuals, the better we can contribute. My recipe is quite simple: **From self-empowerment, to local commitment, to national and global impact.** As you work toward these goals, you will recognize many very important rewards to further inspire you to be an important part of the solution and enjoy the many benefits. Let's create together a great country by strengthening your regional growth. Here are five easy actions we can all take that can have a great positive impact in your community while contributing to your personal betterment:

1. Buy Local: Buying is Voting. Studies reveal that the impact of buying local is tremendous. For example, for a population of one million, if everyone would buy twenty dollars more per week of their local products and services, that would add more than ten thousand new jobs in that community alone! There are numerous rewards for encouraging your local businesses. They contribute greatly in the livelihood of your region. Think about it before you make your next purchase online. Ask yourself these simple questions: Where do the jobs go, where do the profits go, where are the jobs created, where is the return in the local economy? The answer to all these questions is: ELSEWHERE! Consider all the benefits of local purchases. They will most probably make a positive impact for you, your friends, and neighbors. Some rewards to this practice include:

- *Create real job opportunities in YOUR community*
- *Financial impact on local economy: profits, municipal, and state taxes*
- *Create for local businesses the opportunities to prosper and hire*
- *Have the best personalized service*
- *Make your community stronger*
- *Feel good about your positive impact*

2. Local Volunteering: The Many Faces of KINDNESS. Most people associate giving with giving money. I propose an alternative that will cost you nothing and do you so much good: Take the *one day per month volunteering challenge*. Find the right cause and best way to contribute. How can you contribute using your passions and skills and have fun? Imagine if 10 percent of a population of two hundred thousand people would take one day per month for a local volunteering challenge; that would add up to twenty thousand extra productive days per month, totaling two hundred forty thousand per year for helping people in need! Just in your community!

Do you know there are a lot of not-so famous people doing astonishing things too? Ordinary folks who are achieving the extraordinary are out there! We seldom get a chance to see these incredible people. Thanks to CNN Heroes, a beautiful gala held every year, we get to see real-life heroes—people like you and me who are making our world a better place. I'm extremely humbled and moved by the greatness of these individuals who have found an important cause and are doing something about it.

They have become superheroes through helping people and inspiring others to take action. A Spark is what I call any good deed, good idea, kind gesture, and helping hand. In my first book, *The Big Bang Project: Creating Humanity's Best-Case Scenario*, where I bring ideas for a positive future for mankind, I talk about how individuals can be part of the solution. These Sparks are shining a light of hope for mankind. When we hear about a local hero, we are encouraged and inspired. Become a hero yourself, join the Sparks and light up your community and beyond. The list of rewards will surprise you! Here are just a random few:

- *Gratifying feeling of accomplishment*
- *Making new friends who share the same passion*
- *Learning new skills, discovering hidden talents and passions*

- *Contacts and networking helping your career; job opportunities*
- *Bringing a new perspective, appreciating your life and situation*
- *Knowing that you have become a better human being*
- *The pride you feel when seeing how you have impacted the lives of real people*
- *The legacy you leave behind, the values you teach, and the inspiration you bring to your children, friends, and neighbors*
- *The things you learn, the places you go, the people you meet*
- *The future contribution of those you helped may one day help you or a loved one*
- *Avoiding boredom and loneliness, great for uplifting your spirit*
- *It can even fight depression by giving the chance to restart people's lives, ignite a SPARK, and find a new positive purpose*
- *Recognition by family, friends, and community that you are a positive force being part of the solution*
- *Bottom line: better yourself, better your relations, better your career*

Need I say more? The advantages of giving are priceless. Shouldn't it be part of our teens' education? The call to action for good should be learned at a young age. Think of how our world would be different if all children of every school learned a way to participate! Think of the valuable lessons children of both camps would learn! It can be fun to give. What if our children would bring donated stuff that the kids could play with and develop new skills? Musical instruments, Frisbees, books, Rubik's Cubes, and more. Think of the bond the children would develop! A new generation of children who understand the reality of less fortunate people won't judge, but help.

Serving one's country must be about more than joining the army! There are so many possibilities to leave your mark. No need to make it mandatory when all the advantages and rewards speak for themselves.

There are more and more examples of successful career people and celebrities going on to become even better human beings. These influential personalities take charge and contribute by doing good themselves through great organizations they created to directly help people who need our attention. These great positive contributors are what I call "superheroes."

When you give your time and your skills to the community, the positive you give comes back to you in countless ways. This is my best recommendation to begin the positive cycle in your life.

3. Revise Your Personal Behavior: Embrace and Celebrate Diversity. Be open-minded to change on a bigger scale and appreciate and embrace diversity. The **Humble Human Perspective** can be viewed two ways: First, in terms of appreciating our individual uniqueness. Second, in the from of appreciating our social diversity. The personal rewards have a lot to do with self-empowerment. Your positive outlook on other cultures, religions, races, political preferences, social status, and all other differences will bounce right back at you. Here is a short list of important advantages for all of us, starting with you:

- *Learn new perspectives, acquire new knowledge and skills*
- *Focus on issues, not perceptions*
- *Get rid of prejudice and preconceived ideas, discard the negative*
- *Find a consensus based on values and actions rather than culture or faith*
- *Find the positive in everyone, and you can collaborate on common goals*
- *Avoid unnecessary conflicts*
- *Increase your networking, have more friends and allies*
- *Become a "brand of good," be respected by many*

4. Invest in Yourself and Others. Always be open to learn how to better yourself. This will benefit you and those around you. By investing time to teach your know-how, experience, skills, and values to those around you, you also benefit immensely. Here are some of those rewards:

- *Align yourself and close ones with success*
- *Become the expert in your field, gain experience thanks to teaching*
- *Maximize your potential, elevate people you care about*
- *Continuously improve, never be outdated*
- *Build your confidence and personal brand*

5. Be Part of the Movement of Positive Change. Volunteering is one way to make a difference. But being part of a group of people who share their ideas for the common good is another. Imagine how inspiring it can be for so many. Your personal story can inspire more people than you think. Share it! Be inspired by those who will share with you their success stories. Join like-minded people to better your impact and theirs. Sign in at www.thebigbangproject.com. Here are some more personal rewards to consider:

- *Create meaningful relationships*
- *Spread the word and be a positive influence*
- *Be remembered as a positive agent of change*
- *Others will want to join*
- *A better me equals a better we, and vice versa*

As mentioned in the previous chapter, self-empowerment is at its finest expression when you go beyond the "me, myself, and I" quest. Not only will you contribute to your own betterment, you will make a positive impact on others, even possibly our society. So here are ways to be part of the solution by joining forces in groups:

When Positive Forces Unite: A Grand Explosion of Good in Your Neighborhood

My ambitious mission is to trigger our next phase of evolution and begin the process of social repair by igniting a conversation about positive change. We propose new ideas for concrete actions to improve our situation.

Frustration and disillusionment about traditional politics and capitalism have emerged all over the world. This is a sign that for a lot of people the American Dream has become exactly that: a dream. The middle class has been the greatest victim, with opportunities slipping away more and more into the hands of the few rich and powerful.

What if there was a solution allowing the best of you and every community to prevail? What if we could easily remodel our system to bring back opportunity for all? The idea is to recognize there are three spheres of power and influence at work. The first is what I call **individuals and society**, the second is **industries and business**, which represents capitalism (or the right), and the third is the **government** (municipal, state, and national), representing democracy (or the left).

Each of these spheres plays a crucial role in a region's strength. Understanding that they are deeply interconnected and how each can maximize the potential of every community is the next important step. The common denominator of the three spheres of influence is you and me, the people. The following suggestions are meant to empower all of us as individuals working together for a shared goal: *opportunity for all.*

Here's how we can make it happen:

The first sphere (individuals and society) has enormous power and influence. ***We can influence change.*** We elect our politicians to serve us, and we can influence all levels of government to encourage local businesses so that profit stays in our region. Our individual choices and behaviors are at the core of future changes.

If we really want things to change, we can't rely solely on the government or large corporations to solve all our problems. We must do our part and be ready to change for the better. Here are a few ideas to help merge our forces:

Our Mayors

As a citizen, your mayor can be your best contact to make your great idea real. Start on a local level by influencing politicians. This initiative may lead to state and even national improvement.

Our mayors can be our strongest political allies, as they are the closest to the people. Mayors have an enormous power to be the "conductors" of their region's game changers. They can impact the population in more ways than any politicians and influence state and federal political levels. Mayors have the power to inspire positive change through their population's initiatives. By encouraging all positive forces in the region to work together, they can create a positive environment where every entity is part of a common mission: regional strength. This is HUGE!

Chamber of Commerce and Local Businesses

Think of what we can do by working in concert with local businesses, in association with the local chamber of commerce, to provide skills and experience to lift people out of poverty. We can create jobs by asking what products we can produce locally that are presently produced in another country or by an entity with no local ties. We can create a co-op or another type of association or partnership made up of local businesses. Here are two great ideas:

1. ***Create a local brand*** that can be sold by local retailers. The shared profit remains in local hands, creating local jobs.
2. ***Create a regional business website*** offering local retailers and local businesses a Web platform to make it easy for the population to find and buy local.

Banks and large industries are welcome to encourage local growth by financing and partnering with local entities. Politicians of every level can provide the best settings for regional growth by giving incentives for buying local such as no sales tax on locally made products sold where the profit stays in the regions. A form of tax discount could be offered to large entities that partner with local businesses across the country. This represents a positive approach for change. This method is better than the punitive approach presently discussed by politicians. Instead of penalizing importers or outside entities, offer incentives for local purchase. This results in real changes instead of simply giving more income to the government without creating jobs and opportunities.

Buying local makes a great measurable positive impact on the local economy by creating jobs and keeping wealth in the region. This means we must also produce, assemble, and distribute as locally as possible.

NGOs, Associations, Foundations, and Church Groups

Every region already counts many positive contributors from multiple sources. Many people participate actively in making their community a better place. These local heroes are volunteers in nongovernmental organizations (NGOs), foundations, associations, and church groups.

What if instead of working solo or competing with one another, all positive forces joined in the efforts to mobilize the community?

So much can be done by working together for a common goal! Let's create a unified local platform where everyone can participate the way they can by seeing all the possibilities under one roof. Let's create a kindness vibe and make it easy for people to join. Together we can provide for the neediest. We can then integrate them into society by way of education and ultimately help them become productive citizens.

Musicians, Artists, and Athletes

What if we unite through music, art, and sports? Our local artists and athletes can help create a community involvement by all individuals who want to get involved (including immigrants and refugees). This great diversity of people from different cultures, races, and religions can join like never before! Art defies boundaries and breaks language and cultural barriers.

Light up your downtown with creative energy. Downtown streets, where all the merchants have difficulty attracting business, would attract people by letting our artists shine. Make it a place to hang out, where people just want to be! Your local artists would bring a local flavor like nothing else. Let downtown be a place to celebrate safely thanks to music and all our local artists.

Students and Teachers

Your knowledge is precious. Share it with those less fortunate or those having difficulty at school. Not everybody has access to traditional education. But we can make knowledge accessible to all. All you need to do is use social media to share the important lessons you learned, or find a discussion group or a platform of information sharing in a specific topic. You can also volunteer a little bit of your time to help your student colleagues experiencing difficult situations, or find a local organization helping people to learn outside school.

Local Media

The media, might it be local or national, have enormous power. Locally, they can create interest by sharing local positive initiatives. They can spread the good news and mobilize a community. Thank you to all media who keep us informed about our local news and events. *Let's create good news; people need it!*

Let your region shine with a great explosion of good in every neighborhood! Every region should create their own *The Big Bang Project Regional Facebook* page and website, part of a national platform, so that every good idea can be shared nationally. The likelihood that you are part of at least one of these positive forces is enormous. This is the beginning of a great positive movement embracing peace, diversity, fairness, and opportunity for all. Thank you for being part of the solution. Your contribution is precious.

My first book, *The Big Bang Project: Creating Humanity's Best-Case Scenario*, proposes many ideas and solutions to repair our broken democracy and to better realign capitalism to better spread opportunity. Most depict a very negative future for mankind. But I dare to propose a great future for all, **recognizing** that many issues must be requestioned. Then, we can **reset** together by creating a consensus of concrete solutions. Last, we can **reinvent** by making it happen locally and globally.

If we want things to change in our society, we need to accept that we must also evolve as individuals. It all starts with us; a better me for a better we, and vice versa: the ultimate win-win scenario.

Your journey for happiness and success requires discipline and perseverance. *But above all, you must know, believe, and feel that anything is possible when you create your own reality. This is your choice to make.* Now that you possess all the right tools to mold your life the way you want, the rest is up to you.

Thank you for believing in yourself as much as I believe in you.

CONCLUSION
Be the Change You Want to See

There you have it. The message outlined and presented in this book is the result of a lifetime of experience and accumulated knowledge, the totality of which has enabled me to live my dream life to the fullest.

Starting today, you can use the **3R approach** for all issues that are important to you. The resulting success of your reprogramming will last a lifetime. You will constantly reinvent your goals as you reach every single one of them.

You should now be equipped to feel aligned with your own secret through becoming the master of your mind and then the mastermind of your life. Getting out of your comfort zone can eventually become an extraordinarily pleasant habit, similar to following and enjoying your passions.

Once you reach this point, you'll better understand, believe, and feel ready for any challenge. You'll have limitless capabilities.

You have all you need for complete self-reprogramming at the source: your subconscious, heart, and soul. Once you reprogram, you'll be ready to reach the **Perfect Five Alignment: Know it, believe it, do it, feel it, and finally BE IT.**

You can dictate your reality and your future by programming your thoughts and actions at will. This book has helped outline the steps to do that.

If we hope to secure a better world, we must create the perfect environment to strengthen us all to the core. Individuals, families, communities, and regions are the key elements that create a strong country. A strong country can then provide the best opportunity for its citizens to enjoy success and happiness. Our task is to make everyone living within these entities shine to the fullest because we all stand to gain from the success of one another! This is my mission, and it's very clear to me. I hope I have made it clear to you.

Open your mind and your heart to the concepts and ideas proposed in this work. I consider it a great success if I have outlined even one tip to inspire you to rethink the way you are living. It is at least a good starting point for positive change. But before we part, here's my last question and piece of advice:

What's your mission? Well, self-empowerment requires profound introspection. Now that you have this great capacity to mold your thoughts and reality, always aim higher and continue the search for your inner truth. *The best path in finding your life's purpose is to follow your passions.* You are part of the solution in your own way. Find it. Act on it. It represents your soul's bucket list!

Make it more real every day and respect your action plan. *When you think about it, what a great life you have. SO LIVE IT TO THE FULLEST!*

And most important: Enjoy your life because it is the only one you have with this "Avatar."

Luc Goulet, The Leverage Guy

LUC GOULET
The Leverage Guy

Luc has enjoyed great success in every sphere of his life and is now devoted into helping trigger positive evolution for Individuals, Businesses and Foundations, and Society.

From the moment Luc learned how to reprogram his mind at fourteen and got rid of a very heavy stutter in less than three months, he understood how to create his dream life.

Luc joined the family business (Panda Shoes) after college at nineteen, with his brother and sister, they took the business to another level. From just a few stores in Quebec, they franchised across Canada. At 23, Luc had already opened 26 stores from coast to coast. In 2000, the Panda chain counted over 75 stores. Luc was in charge of operations and training franchisees and staff. Panda has won countless awards for best customer service in its category. In 2017, Panda received a "Life Time Achievement Award" by the Retail Council of Quebec (CQCD).

He sold his shares to his partners at 35, to become a full-time dad and husband, and live his passions, while earning his MBA, building a fast growing real estate company, volunteering, and helping businesses of all sizes.

Luc is now embarking in a great journey that started with his first book "The Big Bang Project—Creating Humanity's Best Case Scenario". Enjoying fantastic reviews, Luc is now putting the ideas put forth in his work into action. He is now completing "The Leverage Series" with his third book "Leverage Your Business", after just finishing his second book "Leverage Your Mind".

Living what Luc calls "my soul's bucket list", his life purpose and ambitious mission is to help, with others, trigger our next phase of evolution. He is now devoted in helping people who want to help themselves and others. This includes individuals, local and regional businesses, and all positive forces, such as foundations, Chamber of Commerce, church groups, mayors and even politicians of all levels.

Luc's Vision

"A Better Me for a Better We, and a Better We for a Better Me". Society is made of individuals . . . By empowering people, we create a better society. By helping businesses and all positive contributors we empower communities. By empowering communities we strengthen our country, we then inspire the world for positive change.

The Mission

"From Self-Empowerment, to Local Commitment, for a Global Impact". My mission is to give the tools for people to thrive, to give businesses and all types of organisations new ideas and the best knowledge and plan available. Finally, we must take this historical opportunity to put forth positive ideas to make our country and the world better.

How?

Luc believes in the power of uniting forces with like-minded people and professionals for a greater impact. So, he is creating his every growing "Dream Team" of renowned experts and mentors in all many different fields to join forces on three fronts:

1- Leverage Your Mind—The next phase in Self-Empowerment; www.leverageyourmind.com
2- Leverage Your Business; www.leveragingyourbusiness.com
3- Social Leverage; Leverage Our Social Potential from Local Commitment to Global Impact; www.thebigbangproject.com

The process of positive transformation is possible thanks to Luc's unique and simple "3R For Success" approach:

1- **Recognize** what you want to change, learn the best methods and key factors of success
2- **Reset** your mindset, create the perfect strategy
3- **Reinvent** through action, execute the perfect plan

"Thank you for opening your mind to new possibilities, and for being part of the solution."

The Leverage Guy

LUC GOULET
The Leverage Guy

Email me your comments, questions, and request for services at contact@thebigbangproject.com. Might it be about leveraging your mind, your business or project, or your community, my mission is to help those who want to help themselves or others. Sharing your thoughts can only make my mission improve. All critics are constructive when the intention is improvement.

I very much hope this book helped you have a positive outlook about yourself and your life. Of course, if you want to learn more about becoming a master of your mind and the mastermind of your life or business, I'm happy to help!

I offer my services for individuals and groups, in different possibilities to best fit your needs. Creating the **best-case scenario, recognize, reset,** and **reinvent** your life, business, and community!

Visit my websites for more details:

For self-empowerment: www.leverageyourmind.com
For leveraging your business: www.leveragingyourbusiness.com
For positive social evolution: www.thebigbangproject.com
To know more about Luc Goulet, The Leverage Guy: www.lucgoulet.com

www.ingramcontent.com/pod-product-compliance
Lightning Source LLC
Chambersburg PA
CBHW071737080526
44588CB00013B/2068